Hanna's
Dream Ride

Hanna's

Dream Ride

Hanna Elshoff-Wahlers

ISBN: 978-0-578-93127-2

PUBLISHING COMPANY
Decorah, Iowa

Contents

Acclaim for Hanna's Story

A thoroughly touching tale of Hanna's epic journeys in life. Both her arrival in the USA from Germany in 1961 at age 18, and her bike adventure from Minnesota to Plains, Georgia at age 72 to meet President Jimmy Carter. Along the way she promoted the charity Leader Dogs for the Blind and connected with Lions Clubs, sharing her gratitude to the USA for welcoming her a young immigrant. — *Mike Mesick, M.D.*

Quite winsomely, Hanna Elsoff weaves together a two-year ELF trek with her life story. While set on the roads between Minnesota, Alabama, Georgia, and Washington DC, the story deviates frequently into "daydreams" that open up Hanna's life from Germany to Minnesota. The book is a celebration of accomplishing goals, finding friends anywhere and everywhere, and gratitude for a country that provides a platform for success and kindness. Reading the book is like visiting with Hanna over a cup of coffee." — *Norm Wahl, Ret. Pastor at the Bethel Lutheran Church in Rochester, MN*

Hanna has written a humorous, easy to read book of her adventures of riding her electric cycle and raising money for a very good cause. She is the most adventurous, hard-headed German lady that I have ever meet. She shares the two most important life lessons she has learned of honesty and integrity in her travels and interactions with people. It has been a pleasure to know and work with her. — *George Thompson, Ret. Engineer Manager*

Hanna's story is a delightful read. Her two-year ELF journey was incredible. Now, inspired by Michael Cotter, nationally known Minnesota farmer and storyteller, she has chosen to write of her adventures and to encourage all of us to follow our dream.

— *Bev Jackson Cotter, author, storyteller*

Thank you
To the
United States
Of America
My home

—Hanna Elsoff

A Big Thank You!

Thank you to everyone I met in the two years on the road. In addition, a big thank you to the following people that helped me with straightening out all my writing. The first one, Greta Van Loon, was going to help edit my work. She and her family are very supportive. Then, Dale Heltzer, who is totally blind, had said he had done editing books before and went to work on by book in progress, but it got to be too much for him. Another big thank you to Jan Antonson for bailing me out with the editing. I was just going to have her read some of my book, but she said it was up her alley to edit as she took English in college. When I told her I'd pay her, she said she wouldn't do it for pay. Thanks to my family. They are very supportive with my crazy doings. Silvia, my granddaughter, helped me with the finishing touches of the book and the technical side of things. She kept me in line. And the rest of them, my grandson Armin, my son Karl, my daughter Andrea, and my son-in-law Dan, help and support me. Also, my walking friends, Lori and Susan, help me and talk with me a lot. Dean is a help with computers. Three years ago, when I started my book, everyone was telling me to self-publish it. I said I needed somebody to talk to. I was at Computer Dynamics, a computer repair service store in Chatfield, and Dan, the owner, walked by. He said he knew a publisher in Decorah, Iowa. He gave me the publisher's phone number, and I called him up. I drove to Decorah, and I asked him about publishing a book. That was three years ago. That is how I met Erik Anundsen. He is a great friend to me and was a lot of help.

Everyone I met on the road, absolutely everyone, was supportive, and I am grateful for them. Thank you to all the people who helped me find housing or that housed me. Also, thanks to the people at the motels where I stayed at. They were incredibly great as well. They all started as complete strangers and ended up as friends.

A very special thanks to toastmaster Deanne and her husband Paul Walding. Two weeks before I went on my journey, I arrived at 5 minutes to 7 a.m., Wednesday morning for a Toastmasters meeting. Deanne was already at the meeting. I said to her, "I just got an iPhone." She said, "Hand it to me. We'll put you on Facebook." She asked me a bunch of questions; she said, "What's the name of it?" Off the top of my head, I said, "Hanna's Dream Ride," and it was done. If she would not have done it so quickly, I don't if I ever would have gotten a Facebook page going. Thanks again, and the meeting started.

Opening

Why did I want to do this two-year journey? I didn't have any reason in particular. I just wanted to do it. I was curious to see what the American people were really like. I always felt like they were in general good people. I wanted to thank them and let them know that I was grateful they came to Germany in WWII.

I wished to promote the Lions, especially the Leader Dogs; it is amazing what dogs can do. I also wanted to support the Toastmasters because they have done so much for me.

I never asked for money, but people gave me money anyway. I always told them, "I don't have much, but I have enough." The most touching story was this: I don't remember at all where I was at the time. I was at some gas station. One lady drove up with a dilapidated pickup. She talked to me and admired my ELF. She wanted to give me something. She looked in her purse, and she found a bag of pennies. She said, "Here, you take those." She was very adamant about that. I did and thanked her.

Prologue

The house I was born in

First, before I begin the story of my amazing journey, let me give you some background information, which will help explain some of my feelings and thoughts on my journey. It will also help to show where I began to where I ended up going. Here is where it all started. I was born in this house/barn (they are connected). It was built in 1622 in the village "Borstel," which is near the city, Verden. Verden is located in North Germany close to the North Sea. It was the eighth house built in the village, so we had the house #8. My great-grandfather, Heinrich Rosebrock, bought the farm in 1882. My grandmother, Grete Rosebrock, married Heinrich Wahlers in 1908. They had two children: Tante Mimi and my father, Heinrich (Tante is the German word for aunt). My father was 3 years old when his father was killed in WWI.

My father was 23 years old when he married my mother, Johanna Riemann. Tante Mimi and Uncle Hannes and my parents got married on the same day. The only thing that was wrong on that day was that my mother got very sick. She had pneumonia before they had penicillin. She was so sick she could barely talk, but they got married anyway.

From left to right starting with the top row and finishing with the bottom row, the Wahlers family: Johanne, my mother; Manfred, my brother; Hans-Heinrich, my other brother; Irmgard, my sister; Hanna, me; and Heinrich, my dad.

In 1935, they had their first son, Hans Heinrich. Eleven months later my sister, Irmgard, was born. Manfred came in 1938, and in 1942, in the middle of WWII, I came along.

In 1960, when I was 17, Paul Volker from Fort Dodge, Iowa came to our area of Germany to find his roots. I had a conversation with him. He asked me if I would like to come to America. Well, who wouldn't? He told me that, if my parents gave me permission, he and his wife would help me get a visa. His two children, Judy and Phil, were grown up and married.

When I asked my father, his response in Low German was "gived jo gar nich." In other words, a very strong, "NO WAY."

A month later, after he gave it some thought, he gave me permission unbeknownst to my mother. In 1961, I had all my papers ready and came over on the ship MS BERLIN.

There was a whole train load starting in South Germany with people immigrating to America.

I was on the ship for 10 days. I shared one room with 3 other women. One of them was from East Germany, and she was visiting her sister in New Jersey. When we were in the middle of the ocean, they announced over the speaker that the Berlin wall had been closed. I don't know what that lady did. All I remember is that she cried the rest of the trip. None of us stayed in touch with each other.

One of the days I got sea sick. I don't have a reverse gear. I cannot vomit; I get very, very sick. The captain chased me out of the room. I went on the deck and just laid on a lounge chair. I thought to myself: "If I die, that will be ok." The next day the weather was better and I felt better.

Since Ellis Island was closed six years before I came, the immigration officers came on the ship. Two days before we arrived in New York, a government ferry dropped four immigration officers off onto the ship. A ship is like a hotel on water. Those immigration officers used one of the party rooms as their office.

I left the American consulate in Hamburg where I was given a big manila envelope with all of my immigration papers. It was sealed with a red band and some kind of glue or something. I was not to open it.

We stood in three long lines. We all waited there with each one of us holding our brown envelope. I was so nervous. If one thing was wrong, they would ship me back.

Finally, it was my turn. When the immigration officer got to the negative of my chest x-ray, which was just a little 2 inch square, he looked at it, and then looked at me, and looked at it again. Then he had the other officer look at it. Finally, he gave it to me. I think he got pleasure out of making me more nervous. I still have that negative of my lungs.

It was the last day on the ship at about 10 in the morning. You must remember, I was very naïve and didn't know much at all. Everybody on the deck was looking at something. I looked at the trees and the houses in the distance. I thought it would be totally different. I thought that everything would be upside down on this side of the globe, but it wasn't. Everything was right side up, just like in Germany. Years later, I realized that the people on the deck had been looking at the Statue of Liberty.

A couple that my parents knew and that had immigrated to New York many years before, picked me up from the ship. They took me home. I stayed with them for one night, and they put me on the train to Minneapolis, Minnesota. That's where the Volkers would meet me and take me to Fort Dodge, Iowa.

I didn't know English. All I had was a bicycle to ride. A couple of years later, I had connections in Texas. I was footloose and fancy free. I was going to ride my bike to Texas like a hobo. If it took two years, it wouldn't matter. When I told my sponsors, the Volkers about my dream, they said that it was too dangerous. I did go to Texas a few years later, but not on a bike.

I never gave up on that dream!

Life took me in all kinds of directions. When I went to Texas, I stayed for several years and met my future husband there. He was in the military. We got married and moved to Rochester, Minnesota, which was his hometown. We had two children.

In 1971, my father sent my bachelor brother over to buy a farm. Manfred bought a farm in Chatfield. After one year, our parents came to see him and the farm. Manfred got homesick. He said, "I have to go back with you, or I will die." My father asked me to take care of the farm. Manfred went back to Germany, and I took care of the farm from there. That's how I got to Chatfield, Minnesota.

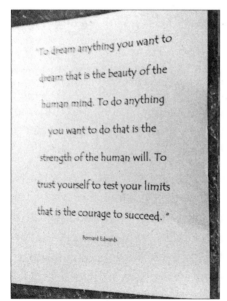

"To dream anything you want to dream that is the beauty of the human mind. To do anything you want to do that is the strength of the human will. To trust yourself to test your limits that is the courage to succeed."

Bernard Edwards

THE DREAM!

If I was going to live my dream, I needed to be out of debt. I shouldn't have had any responsibilities. I was thinking, perhaps, when I am eighty years old, if I live that long, I'll be footloose and fancy free, AGAIN.

On my seventieth birthday, I realized that my responsibilities were getting close to ending. I had joined the Lions club. I could use that to my advantage. I could get away when I was seventy-five. That gave me five years to plan my DREAM RIDE.

Two years into it, I saw a bike with a motor at Menard's in Rochester. I thought, "I am not in that good of shape; I need a bike with a motor."

One evening I was sitting in front of the computer. I was wondering if there is such a thing as a solar powered bike. I entered "solar powered bike" in the computer and up came a bike called ELF made in Durham, NC.

I am kind of spontaneous. I had frequent flyer miles. I flew to Durham, NC. I rode one of those solar powered bikes and I ordered one for myself.

In May 2014, while I was in Durham, I decided, "I am not going to wait until I am 75 years old. I am going to leave May 1st, 2015." That gave me one year to make my plan.

AND THAT IS WHAT I DID.

I had a few definite destinations: a high school graduation of Caleb VanLoon in Rochester in June of 2015, and the Lions US-Canada Leadership Forum on September 17, 2015. After that, I would head south to meet Jimmy Carter. The rest of the time, I would go wherever fate took me.

Minnesota

This book is written in sequence starting May 1st 2015 through May 11th 2017.

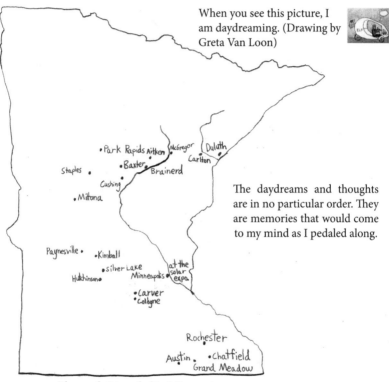

When you see this picture, I am daydreaming. (Drawing by Greta Van Loon)

The daydreams and thoughts are in no particular order. They are memories that would come to my mind as I pedaled along.

The roads I traveled in Minnesota

Friday, May 1, 2015

I am 72 years old and I am going on a 2 year journey. It has been my dream for fifty years, and today is the day!!!

It is 10:00 AM. My solar powered tricycle is packed. I have been working and planning a whole year for this journey.

I am leaving the driveway and I turn left. My daughter, Andrea, is working in the garden. She comes running and takes a quick picture.

My neighbor, Frank Bailey, who passed away some years ago, said that we lived on the highest point of Olmsted county. I don't know if that is true, but the road I am riding on is hilly and curvy. In four miles the road comes to a "T." On the left is the Orion township cemetery. Oh my, now my thoughts are going wild.

 Citizenship

I got my American citizenship in 1978, but I could have gotten it much sooner. I told everybody that I was a happy ALIEN.

It was Jimmy Carter that inspired me to work on my citizenship.

One day, the TV was on as I was walking past, and I heard someone saying, "I am an American farmer, and I am running for President!" I thought to myself: A farmer, running for president? Only in America!

I wanted to vote for him, but I couldn't because I was not a citizen.

I put everything in gear to get my papers so that I could vote for him. I eventually got my citizenship papers, but not in time to vote for President Carter. There was also one other thing wrong. When you get naturalized as a citizen, you get a big manila envelope with a pamphlet, some little booklets, and a letter from the president of the United States of America, who at that time was President Jimmy Carter. I read the letter welcoming me as an American citizen, but it was signed by Gerald Ford, not Jimmy Carter. I imagine that no one else noticed it, but I did. I thought to myself: someday, I am going to get the signature of President JIMMY CARTER above Gerald Ford's. Now I am a citizen of the United States of America!

I immediately and proudly applied for an American passport, which I had to use a few years later to visit Germany because my father was in poor health. On the way back to the U.S.A., we got off the plane at the International Airport in Chicago. We were greeted by an African American gentleman who said, "WELCOME HOME." That really touched me, and then I had the privilege to stand in line with the American citizens, which also really got to me. I looked around and wondered how many people

were as lucky as I? How many people were going home; HOME to Minnesota, HOME to Chatfield, on top of the hill where the wind blows?

I looked around to see if anyone was watching as tears were running down my cheeks. Why is it, when tears run, the nose starts running too? I was a mess. I always liked it here, but it had never before felt like my home. When I went to Germany, it definitely didn't feel like home anymore. But now, now that I was an American citizen, I felt like I truly belonged here, like I was HOME! THANK YOU AMERICA!!!!!

What makes a person feel at home? Is it the weather? The scenery is beautiful around Chatfield certain times of the year, it's true. However, I say it is the people that make one feel at home. People like Betty and Lowell Wooner, who drove by every Sunday morning and stopped to visit. Frank Bailey also stopped and visited: Helen and Wally Mercer did, too. The business people in Chatfield, like Palmer and Audrey Borgen, treated me well; and the list goes on.

 Cemetery

Now that I was part of the USA, I wanted to be buried in this country; in Chatfield, in the Orion township cemetery at the end of our MILL CREEK ROAD. I had quite a time finding out who I needed to talk to buy a plot. I asked all of the neighbors. One of them thought that I should ask Jim Burnap. Well, he was the guy. Jim and Carolyn are also farmers. Thy live about eight miles from where I live. He was going to meet me on Sunday at 1:00 in the afternoon. I told our neighbors that if they wanted to buy a cemetery lot, I was going to meet Jim Burnap at 1:00 PM on Sunday. Three couples showed up; Wally and Helen Mercer, who have already passed away; Betty and Lowell Wooner, who also are gone; and the Mercers best friends, the Hinzmans. Today, the Hinzmans and myself are the only ones left.

These seven people showed up that Sunday afternoon. Jim came with what looked like a scroll. It was an old window shade from the late 1800s, with cemetary plots drawn on it. We all picked out a spot. The price? One hundred dollars for mine, and two hundred for a double spot (mowing included). We finished our purchases and everyone went home happy.

I had enough money left that I could afford to put a headstone on my piece of property, so I went to the small town of Lewiston to purchase a headstone.

The salesman showed me a few different ones. I picked out a light gray one. We went in the office to see what I wanted written on it. He showed me a book with pictures. Since I believe in angels, I chose an angel on each side, one angel on the right and one on the left. I wanted my name, "Hanna" on the top in the middle. Everyone in Chatfield knows that crazy German woman on top of the hill. Then I said: "I've been divorced for a long time. My married name is 'Elshoff'; I never changed it back. My maiden name is Wahlers, so I want 'Wahlers' after 'Elshoff.'" "I was born in 1942. I have many things planned," I said, counting them off on my fingers. "I have to live to be one hundred and ten years old. So, 1942 plus 110; that brings it to 2052." I wanted them to put 1942-2052 for my birth and death dates on my headstone. The salesmen gave me a blank look. I said, "You've never had that request before? Doesn't everybody have a plan?" He replied, "What if it doesn't happen? You know it's in stone." I said, "Who cares? I won't be around anyway."

That's how I left it. I don't remember how much I paid for that headstone, but I think it was about five hundred dollars. As I walked out I said with a smile, "No need to hurry, you know."

The stone showed up about two months later. The dates are right on there; 1942-2052.

A few months later Pam Davidson's grandmother was buried not far from my plot. Pam told me that at the burial, pretty soon no one was listening to the preacher. Jim Riley, the undertaker, looked at that date on my headstone. He looked the headstone over. He looked behind it. He said, "It looks like it came from Lewiston Monument. I can't imagine that they would ever make that kind of mistake." Someone else popped up and said, "She is still alive, I just saw her the other day."

It has been about twelve years since the headstone showed up. Now everybody knows that I am a little nutty. There is a reason my father let me come to the USA: They didn't have any use for me in Germany.

I am a late bloomer; I'm just budding now that I am in my seventies.

I joined Toastmasters over thirty years ago. Toastmasters helps a person overcome the fear of speaking in front of an audience. They say that it's the biggest fear, bigger than the fear of death. Well, I am not afraid of dying but I did have a terrible fear of talking in front of people. I could not even say my name. I was milking cows at that time and listening to the radio in the barn. I heard a lady named Marie Pesch say to an interviewer, "Overcome the fear of speaking and join Toastmasters!"

After two years of searching to find out about Toastmasters, a good friend of mine, Linda Ottmann, who worked at the Mayo Clinic called me. "You wanted to know about Toastmasters? There is an article in the clinic magazine. Here is the phone number." (Linda died a few years ago from cancer, and I miss her a lot.)

In Toastmasters they have speech contests. In the fall, it's a humorous speech contest. No one in our club would volunteer to be a contestant. Well, I thought; maybe I could talk about my headstone. It was somewhat funny.

On the tenth of October 2008, I had made it to the third level of the contest. The contest took place in Frontenac, Minnesota. In the middle of the speech, I began to talk like a drunk. I don't remember anything after that. I was having a stroke. It certainly wasn't funny for the audience, but I still think it is funny. I was talking about my cemetery plot, and I nearly kicked the bucket right there on stage. I vividly can remember thinking; I am going to die; I am not going to make 110; it's ok, just relax...

My final destination
The final date is only my plan.

Obviously I am still alive, and I am supposed to write this book!
I am done daydreaming for now. Back to the road…

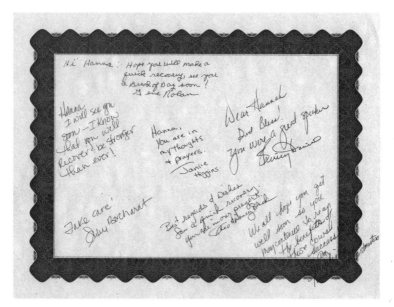

These are all the people at the speech contest that
watched me fall over backwards.

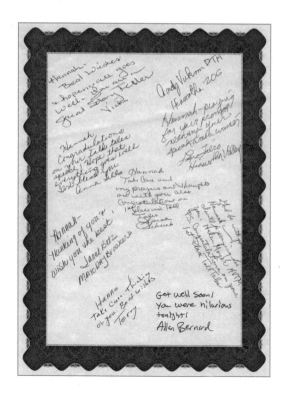

I have to turn right onto County Road 7. I ride on a black top road for about a mile. Then I turn left onto a gravel road again. I had my bike a year before I went on my journey. I go past a turkey farm. I have taken this trip several times to Rochester. Usually a dog comes running from the farm, but not this time. I think he hurt himself last time. He never knows where to attack me and ran his head into the ELF. I hope it didn't kill him. I'm sure he had a headache.

I take a right, and then a left onto Highway 52. I have to concentrate on this road. It's a very busy road, with car after car zooming past. It has a good wide shoulder. After about two miles, I take the right exit onto Marion Road.

 Earth Day

I got a call from a lady who was going to be at an Earth Day Celebration on the Sunday morning a week before I was to leave on my journey. She asked me if I could bring my solar powered bike there. "Yes, I can do that," I said. I had to be there by 10:00 AM. I left at 7:00 AM. It was about 20 miles. I had ridden that stretch a number of times.

On Saturday, the day before the Earth Day Celebration, Hannah from the Austin TV station called. She wondered if she could meet me in Rochester the next day for an interview and I agreed.

Hannah came with her parents as a child from Vietnam.

We met on Sunday morning, across from Cubs grocery store. Hannah and I "Hanna" went in the parking lot. Hannah did a lot of work. I never saw the TV interview, but I imagine it was good.

When I got to the Mayo Civic Center, the site of the Earth Day Celebration, they were looking for me. Some guy stopped me and told me that he had seen an article about me in the paper, and that he was a fan of Jimmy Carter. At the same time, some women were hollering at me "Hanna, you are late. You have to give a speech." Ralph Kahler from the Solar Energy Company that was building the solar panels on the farm for me had asked me to give a talk at the Earth Day Celebraton about my journey and a little bit about the bike and solar energy.

After the talk, they escorted the ELF and me to the front door of the building, right at the entrance. That ELF got a lot of attention. A young man

came from KTTC TV in Rochester. He talked to me for a long time. I told him that I was going next week on my two year journey. The Rochester Lions were having a send-off at the Bethel Lutheran church for me at 9:00 AM." I will be there," he said.

That evening, because it was getting dark, a former foster daughter and her husband picked me up with a trailer and took me back home.

I HAD AN EXITING DAY !!!!

Back to my journey...

Marion road is nice. I am riding to meet fellow Lion, Rich Jersa. He and another Lion, Steve Gilseth, will be riding on regular bikes to Fort Dodge, Iowa with me.

Rich doesn't live too far away from the Bethel Lutheran Church. I am staying overnight at Jon and Lori'house. They live south of Rochester, close to the air port. Rich will take me in his car to Jon and Lori's house (I was their nanny for many years).

Saturday, May 2, 2015

Today is the second day of my journey. Jon will take me back to Rich's house at 7:00 AM. Rich and I will ride our bikes to Bethel Lutheran Church where the BIG, SENSATIONAL SEND-OFF will take place.

We get there about 8:00 AM. Steve shows up as well. The pastor makes coffee and the Hy-Vee grocery store supplies the sweet stuff. People start to come. It's a big event. My family comes, including my son, Karl, from Winona. I am guessing there were about 100 people in all. The Rochester Mayor gave a talk. The young man from KTTC is here. He even interviews Armin, my grandson. It is very nice. At 10:00 AM, it is time to go. We have a police escort. Rich and Steve holler at me, "Come on, Hanna. The policeman is stopping the traffic!" We cross the road and we are on our way.

Just a short stretch and we are on the bike trail. I just follow the guys. Both Rich and Steve are avid bike riders, they know their way around.

We ride on the trail for about an hour. We get to the end of it, and who is there? The police. I say to them, "You don't have to escort us anymore." "Oh yes," the policemen said," I was asked to make sure you get to the county line safely." "Oh, well, I guess that will be okay." Just then, 6 or 7 bicycle riders come toward us. They are interested in the gadget I'm riding. They have a lot of questions for me and I gladly answer them. They are so interested in my story and why I have planned the trip for two years. This is only my second day!

Next, we ride toward Grand Meadow to Lion Past District Governor Clair and Carol Mrotek's. They had invited us to spend the night at their house. The two guys sleep outside in their tents. Although Rich had given me a tent, I got to sleep in the house.

Sunday, May 3, 2015

After a beautiful breakfast, we continue on our way to Austin, Minnesota. The ride is pretty uneventful. We get to Austin and meet District Governor Jim Dunlop at the park. After that, we go to Ed and Ruth Aron's. Almost a year ago, at the Lions Peace Poster Contest, Ruth invited me stay with her when on my journey. I took her up on the invitation. I called her. I will have to explain to Ruth that I have two guys along, but that she shouldn't worry: they have their own tents.

When we get to their house, the guys start to set up their tent. Ruth tries to talk them into staying in the house. "No, no we can sleep in the tent." "Well," Ruth says, "If you get wet, you can't come in the house." That convinces them to sleep in the house. What a good idea that was. In the evening we go to a Lions meeting in Lyle. The meeting has to be cut short because a big storm is starting. It is almost tornado-like. The tents would have been hanging in the trees.

In conversation with Ruth, I tell her that I have forgotten one thing. I didn't bring a journal with me. I have the iPhone, but I don't really know what to do with it yet. Ruth says, "Just a minute. I had a garage sale, so let me look and see if there is something you can have." She comes back with a book called "Kiss and Tell." It is a funny book, which is just up my alley. (Thank you, Ruth, for your motherly advice.)

Monday, May 4, 2015

Off to Iowa. Past District Governor Earl and Jane Orvik had made arrangements for accommodations for us from there on up to Fort Dodge. Later on, he also helped me out in Minnesota. (Thanks again, Earl and Jane.)

The weather has been pretty good to us up until now. After the bad storm last night, we have a lot of wind to deal with. The terrain is very flat, mostly corn and soybean fields. It must be hard to pedal a regular bike. It's not bad for me, I have a motor. I have two big batteries to help. One battery lasts for 30 miles on an average day. On a windy day, it's a lot less. Today we have about 50 miles to ride. The guys stay right behind me. The ELF breaks the wind for them. Soon it is time to switch the battery. We stop in the middle of nowhere. The guys have to rest, but I am fine. I unplug the one battery and plug in the second battery. All is fine. Then I push the power button on the handle bar, and nothing happens-no power.

What to do?

AAA, at this time, does not service bikes. Organic Transit in Durham, North Carolina, that built the bike, partnered with "Better World" (Compares to AAA) and they gave me a year's subscription.

I take out my wonderful phone and plan to give them a call. It is so darn windy that I am unable to hear anything. There is a house a long way from the road. The guys are lying in the ditch and resting, so I walk to the house. No one is home. I find a corner where the wind isn't blowing so hard so that I can hear better. I get ahold of Better World. I tell them that I have a solar powered bike from Organic Transit.

I switched batteries and now it won't run. About half an hour or more passed. I go to the guys and tell them that Better World will call me back when they find a truck to pick us up and take us to a bike shop. I say, "I can still ride it; I can always pedal. It is pretty flat ground. The pedals always work." The guys are rested. We start going, I push on the power button and suddenly everything works.

I call Better World and cancel the service call.

We get to Lion Mike Blaeckmoer's in Mason City, Iowa late in the afternoon. I immediately plug both batteries into the charger. It takes about six hours for one battery to charge.

Mike says, "There is an ELF in Mason City; owned by an attorney. He rides his bike to work every day. I'll give him a call. He can stop by after work."

Later, that attorney stops by. It's funny to see two ELFs sitting in the driveway. The guy is nice but I didn't get to say very much. He must have something special with that company, ORGANIC TRANSIT, because he is bragging about how he has the twelfth bike that they built. He has only one battery so he can not help me with my problem. He says that he never pedals, he only uses the power.

We have a beautiful supper. Mike's wife, Michelle, comes home later. We visit a little and then go to bed.

I have them write in the book that I got from Ruth, "Kiss and Tell." There are some nice sayings in the book. This is one of them:

'If you're lucky, you have a kiss or two worth remembering. Maybe it was a quick peck on the dance floor.'

Or a passionate kiss on the beach under the moon. Or a sloppy kiss from a two year old as you put him down for a nap.

Wherever it was, whenever it was, chances are, that kiss changed you for the better. Because every good kiss (and even the occasional bad one) reminds you that you're human. That you're not in this life alone. And most important, that you are someone worth kissing, which is a wonderful thing to be, when you really think about it. XOXO THE EDITORS'

Tuesday, May 5, 2015

We are on the way to Hampton, Iowa. Our next host will be Elaine Wilcox. It's another 50 to 60 mile day. It's still windy, but not as bad as yesterday.

After about 25 miles, the same thing as yesterday happens: I have to switch batteries. Wouldn't you know–no power again. The only difference is, in the middle of nowhere, there is a big factory and all of the doors are wide open. People are walking around. I ride my bike right through the big doors. Of course, they are all interested in the contraption. I tell them what the problem is. Six or seven guys come and they start working on it. Rich and Steve sit on steps somewhere. The guys plug in the electric cord and there is no power. I leave the men alone and look for Rich and Steve. When I find them, Rich says, "Let's abort this trip." They let us use the board room for us to make phone calls home. We were just about to make the first call when one of the guys walks in and says "Everything is working. The extension cord was bad."

It is wet and cold and still windy but when one pedals, one gets warm in a hurry. I am way ahead of the guys. It is about 4:00 PM. An SUV comes toward me as I am reaching the town of Hampton. A lady sticks her head out and says, "You must be Hanna, I am so glad to see you! I was so afraid you were going to be here earlier. I was at the doctor's office and got a shot for pain. I had to wait there for an hour to make sure I didn't have a reaction. Boy, I am glad to see you." Her name is Elaine. She points across the street to a church. "Ride over there, the newspaper and radio people are coming to interview you."

A little while later the two guys arrive, all exhausted. They ride into the church parking lot, sit down and wait until the interviewing is done. Steve says to Elaine, "We want to take you and Elaine out to eat." "No, no," Elaine says, "I have a roast in the oven; and potatoes and vegetables are cooked. You eat at my house. My husband died a year ago and this is the first meal I have cooked. You are my first company I am having."

She is very happy! I think that we are supposed to be here. We have a very good time with Elaine, and it is an excellent meal.

Wednesday, May 6, 2015

Elaine has to go to work at 8:00 AM. We left at the same time as she. It is very foggy. We go to Hardee's and stay there until the fog lifts. In the meantime, I walk to the bank were Elaine works and I have some copies made. Elaine introduces me to all of her coworkers. It's all so wonderful. I get back to Hardee's. The fog had lifted. We go on with our journey.

Clarion is our next destination. It starts to get really windy, wet and cold. We have only 30 miles to go, but in this kind of weather that is far enough. Again, the guys stay right behind me so I can break the wind. Every once in a while one of them hangs on to the back of my bike to give himself a little boost. That works pretty well. At last, we get to Clarion. In Clarion we stay in a motel.

Thursday, May 7, 2015

In the morning, we continue on our way to Fort Dodge. It's about 40 miles, not too bad of a distance.

I am far ahead of the guys and the weather is much better today. I approach a fork in the road and I need the guys to tell me which way to go. I wait by the railroad tracks. After a while, Steve shows up. He asks, "Did you see Rich?" "I thought he was with you." "No," Steve says," I haven't seen him either."

We wait for quite a while. Finally Steve says, "I am going to look for him." After about a half an hour he comes back with the news: a lady had stopped and told him that she saw a guy pushing a bike. Steve had decided to come back and wait with me, but now he decides to go into an office building that is across the street.

The office building has a big parking lot and a grassy area. Steve walks inside and tells them the dilemma we're in. He also asks if we can sit and wait on the grass for Rich and if we can use their bathroom facilities. "Of course," they tell us, "The men are all out with their big equipment working."

We wait for a long time. Finally Rich comes along, pushing his bike. He sits down with us in the grass and tells us his sad story. He had gotten a flat tire. He changed the inner tube, got on and rode just a few feet before it went flat again. He didn't want to risk his last new inner tube, so he had pushed the bike the rest of the way.

After telling us what happened, he takes the wheel off and takes the tire apart to see if there is anything that could have punctured the inner tube. We don't find a thing. Rich puts it all back together with his last new inner tube. Then he goes over to the shop to use the compressor. I walk behind him, carrying his tools. He has the tire sitting on a barrel and is putting air into it. I say, "Just be-" but before I can finish, puff! The tire blows up.

Well…… That's the end for us for today. We were trying to get to Fort Dodge where Steve's wife is visiting with her daughter and playing with the grandchildren. She has come a day early with the pickup truck. I say, "This is simple; just call her and she can pick you up here in Eagle Grove." Rich is very upset that he caused the problem again. "What do you mean, again?" I ask. "Well that's a long story," he replies.

Steve and Rich push their bikes about four or five blocks to the next gas station. I ride around town to see if they have a motel. I find one not far from the gas station and get a room for myself. I go back to the gas station and we all have something to eat. The guys are surprised that I have already found a motel and gotten a room. They say that they were just about to feel sorry for me that I had nowhere to go.

Steve's wife, Laurie, comes and picks them up and they go to Fort Dodge. I ride my bike back to the motel. Lion Earl Orvik had given me the name of a Lions District Governor in this area. She lives right in Eagle Grove. It is about noon and we haven't gotten very far. I call her up and ask if she could meet me. We meet in a restaurant. She says she will try to get the club together for this afternoon.

Like a miracle worker, she gets a whole lot of people together and we have a great evening. In addition, she offers to come in the morning and escort me out of town. (Her name is Andrea, but she goes by Andy).

Friday, May 8, 2015

Andy shows up right on time at 7:00 AM and I am ready to go. Not only does she escort me out of town, but she escorts me all the way to Fort Dodge. The weather is pleasant and we have a great ride. At about 10:00

AM we get to the motel in Fort Dodge. We say our goodbyes with lots of hugs.

A very big thanks to Andy!!!

The Past District Governor, along with Lion Timothy Wilson, meets me at the motel. The Lions had made the reservations for me.

Fort Dodge was my very first stomping grounds in this country in 1961. Since then, they have built a Federal Prison where the prisoners train leader dog puppies from Rochester Hills, Michigan. It is a tremendous program which helps the prisoners and the dogs, but mostly the prisoners. They did a documentary on it a few years ago. Warden Jim McKinney started the program. It is totally incredible.

I RECOMMEND FOR YOU TO SEE IT. YOU CAN FIND IT ON GOOGLE: PRISON PUPPY PROGRAM , FORT DODGE, IOWA

OR AT: "LEADER DOG FOR THE BLIND PRISON PUPPY RAISNG PROGRAM" on you tube. This you should really watch.

I am going to pedal around in Fort Dodge. The people that sponsored me, Paul and Clarabelle Volker, have both died. I will find where I lived with them. I'll go to the hospital where I worked. Among other things, I will enjoy myself.

Lion Tim has organized a meeting with the Fort Dodge Lions. That is always fun and enjoyable.

I get a call on my first day in Fort Dodge from George Thompson, a Toastmaster member from Rochester, Minnesota. He and his wife are on their way to

My sponsers for my immigration Visa in 1961, Clarabel and Paul Volker

Missouri, and they will stop by to see me. That is very exciting for me. We had a great visit.

 Solar Expo

What happened after Fort Dodge is a little bit of a complicated story.

Last winter, I sold some trees out of the woods on the farm. They were mostly walnut trees. They were the highest price in history at that time. I got, in my opinion, a big chunk of money for these trees. I had to pay 30% capital gain taxes, which I really didn't want to do. I decided to convert the wood into solar panels; giving myself 30% tax credit.

I found somebody through Rehm and Zola up in the twin cities. His name is Ralph Kahler from St. Charles, Minnesota. He came to talk to me. When he saw my ELF with the solar panel, he got very excited. For the first three hours, we talked about my bike and my journey. He said, "Can you come to a Solar Expo in Minneapolis?" "When is it?" I asked. He looked in his calendar. "The 15th of May." After I looked in my calendar and saw that Earl had nothing scheduled for me after Fort Dodge, Iowa, I replied, "Yes." Ralph told me, "I can pick you up wherever you are and take you wherever you need to go afterwards." After we had all of that settled, he talked for 30 minutes about the solar panels I was interested in. At about noon he said, "Well, I have to go now. I'll figure it out and let you know what price it will be. You will hear from me in a few days. By the way, can you give a talk at that expo?" Well, that was a bit out of my comfort zone, but I belong to Toastmasters, so I told him, "I can do that."

Back to my journey in Fort Dodge!

I stay for two nights in Fort Dodge, enjoying riding around with my ELF. It's interesting to see the Lutheran hospital. It has totally changed over fifty years. I find where I lived, 227 9th Ave N. I don't know why that address suddenly pops into my head. It all seems so different now. Nevertheless, it is fun.

Sunday, May 10, 2015

I get picked up by my former foster daughter and her husband (Janelle and Kevin) with their enclosed trailer. They take me home to get ready to go to Minneapolis on the 14th of May for the Solar Expo.

I raised Janelle as a foster child since she was 11 years old. She stayed with me. When she and Kevin got married, they put a mobile home next to the house. They have helped a lot on the farm ever since then.

Thursday, May 14, 2015

Ralph Koehler picks me up promptly at six in the morning and we are on our way to Minneapolis to the Solar Expo. It's about a two hour drive. We arrive at one of the fanciest Hotels in downtown Minneapolis. I push the ELF to the entrance and a number of doormen open the door for us. I feel like some kind of celebrity. We need to get to the second floor. We try to get the ELF in the elevator, but it doesn't fit. "There's a double door," Ralph says. It's a door into the kitchen. Everybody here is very nice, and they kindly push stuff out of the way for us. Unfortunately, it doesn't get us anywhere. Ralph was hoping for a freight elevator with indoor access, but we have no such luck. I finally just hand the bike over to Ralph. Embarrassed, I walk away like I have nothing to do with that thing.

We walk outside, down the sidewalk and around the corner to the freight elevator. Ralph pushed the ELF; I walked behind like a lost person.

When we get to the second floor, there are all the people with their solar goods. Everyone is all dressed up in suit and tie. I am in my "dress uniform," which is not as fancy. Oh, well, that's the way it is. In no time, I am surrounded by all of the salespeople. Ralph goes about his own business, looking around and talking to people. This is very exciting for me. Soon, the ELF is the main attraction. I am supposed to speak at noon at the luncheon. I am getting so nervous, I feel like I am going to have another stroke. By 11:00, I have to go to a quiet corner and settle down a little. Finally Ralph comes back and says we have to go to the luncheon.

The dining room is beautifully decorated. We are seated close to the stage, where a lady is currently talking about the solar panels she was promoting. It sounds a bit boring. I can't pay a whole lot of attention to what anybody is saying. I can't even eat anything. Then comes my turn. Ralph introduces me, which is helpful. He tells them that I am going to talk about coming from Germany, the Lions, and the prison puppy program.

Now it is time for my ten minute speech!

I step onto the stage.

"A little while ago one of you guys asked me if I was selling that thing, the ELF, and I said 'Ahh...no.' Then came the question, 'are you representing a company?' Again I said, 'Ahh...no.' Then he asked, 'What are you doing here?' I raised my arms up and said, 'I have no idea, what I am doing up here. What I do know is that all of you better start selling those solar panels fast and furiously. They're drilling into our earth deeper then I think is good for us. They are doing something called fracking. Pretty soon we will all be falling into a big hole, and then we won't need anything."

Next I tell them a little bit about coming to America and a little about Toastmasters, how it helps everybody to communicate better. I talk about belonging to Lions, and how it gives everyone a purpose. I tell them how they started the Leader Dogs for the Blind in Rochester, Michigan, and the prison puppy program in Fort Dodge, Iowa.

Before I knew it, my ten minutes are up.

I sit down with my elbow on the table and my head between my hands and say quietly, "Thank GOD that is over with." The next thing I know, someone is tapping me on the shoulder. I barely look at him as he says, "That was the best speech we have heard all day." Then he taps on my shoulder again and says, "You're the only one that got a standing ovation." I think I said thank you, but everything after that is sort of a blur.

Ralph and I load the ELF back on the trailer and we take off to Carver, Minnesota.

I had called Earl when I found out that I was going to be in Minneapolis and asked him if he could find a place outside of Minneapolis. He had called me back and gave me a number for Kristy in Carver, Minnesota.

We get there at about four o'clock in the afternoon. Ralph leaves to go home. I scope out the town just a little bit, and find a restaurant/bar. When Kristy called me to tell me that I can stay at her house, she told me that she is playing volleyball and that she won't be home until 6:30. I told her she can find me at the bar in town.

I am well entertained in this bar. Lots of people are coming and going. My ELF is the big attraction, as usual. No one has ever seen anything like it. At 7:00, Kristy arrives. She knows right away who I am. She puts her arms around me and says "When they told me how old you are, I thought of my grandmother. She died in my arms a year ago."

Kristy and her friend, Andy, escorted me to Kristy's house. We visited for a while, and then went to bed.

Friday, May 15, 2015

I'm still in Carver, Minnesota. Andy has to be at work really early, 5:00 in the morning. Kristy has to be at the bank at 8:00. I tell her that I'll leave when she leaves. Quite a few people show up outside at the town hall at about 9:00, including the newspaper guy with his camera. Marvin from the Carver Lions Club escorts me to Anna Wickenhauser's house. This is a good thing, because they live a long ways out in the countryside of Cologne, Minnesota. I think for a while that we'll never get there. Marvin is surprised at how fast I always catch up with him. He says he just got the newspaper out and there I am again. With pedaling and the electric power I can go close to twenty miles per hour. A guy on a regular bike can go that fast with no help, but not I. I can probably go ten miles an hour on my own, on a good day.

Anna, her husband, Don and some of the kids welcome us. Marvin stays to talk a few minutes and goes home. We go inside; they have a very big house. They show me my room downstairs.

It's 2:00 in the afternoon. They are getting ready for graduation. Anna's mother is there, helping with painting. I roll up my sleeves and ask if I can do anything. "Oh yes, if you want to help, we have work for you," she replies. I feel at home. Later in the evening, we have supper. After visiting awhile, I go to bed.

Saturday, May 16, 2015 – Cologne, Minnesota

This is the first full day at Anna Wickenhauser's family home. Anna has planned a party in my honor.

She invited the Lions club.

At about the same time Carrie Steidl calls. She's wondering where I am and if I have started my journey. I tell her that I am in Cologne. "We don't live far from there. Is there a way we can come and see you?" she asks. I give the phone to Anna. Anna invites her to the party in my honor. When she hangs up, she says, "One or ten more, it doesn't matter."

 How I met the Steidls

Now you wonder how I met Steidl's. The year before I went on my journey, I rode the bike around to see how many miles I could ride comfortably in one day. I was still working overnights at Madonna Towers Independent, Assisted Living and Nursing Home, therefore I had limited time. I rode the bike to Lewiston, MN and left it at a fellow Lion's house. They gave me a ride back to Chatfield. After a few days, I drove my car back to Lewiston, left it there and rode the bike to Winona. I left the bike at Lion friends, Sue and Jack Krage's house for a few days. They took me back to Lewiston, where I picked up my car and went home. After a few more days, I drove to Krag's house and rode my bike to Kellogg, Minnesota. On my way to Kellogg, I went on the bike trail in Winona. That's where I met the Steidl's. They were on their way to Iowa and had stopped for lunch with their two children. As I got closer, they started talking to me. I stopped and conversed with them. The kids rode the bike and had a good time. I talked to the parents and told them about my journey that I

had planned starting May first 2015. Ted Steidl invited me to their house when I am on my journey. I didn't make it to their house. Actually, I had forgotten about them.

That's how I met the STEIDLE'S!

Now back to Wickenhauser's in Cologne......

In the afternoon we go to a school festival, which is lots of fun and gives me ideas for what we can do in Chatfield.

Sunday, May 17, 2015

It's a big day. Anna has so much energy. She has prepared all of the food for the party. Many people show up. They are mostly Lions, including Ted Steidl and his wife and children. Ted Steidl's sister lives in Miltona right on my way to Park Rapids. He tells us that you don't need to be afraid to go there. Their house is open to anyone. He and his wife are both Lions.

Monday, May 18, 2015

Anna has organized a Leo club, which is a Lions Club for teens. This is a huge undertaking. The Leo's meet on Monday evenings at the school. We go there and I am very impressed.

Anna does another thing for me: she organizes places for me to stay all the way to Miltona, MN. It is about 170 mile from Cologne. She makes call after call until she finds a Lion that is willing to house me. She has the names all written down, all the towns and phone numbers. It is really great for me. Thank you again Anna, for all you did for me!!!

Tuesday, May 19, 2015 – Silver Lake, Minnesota

Tuesday morning, fairly early, I am on my way to a town called Silver Lake. I will be staying with Duane and Lynn Yurek. It starts out weather-wise pretty good. As I ride, it gets a little nasty. I have only 30 miles to go. Ordinarily, that's not too much, but I am bucking the wind. I'm going through a little town. Pretty soon a pickup is beside me. I stop, and he says, "I am a Lion. You drove by where I work. I just happened to be outside. I saw your Lions flag on your...whatever you call that thing you're riding.

I figured you must be a Lion." "I'm going to Silver Lake," I tell him. He says, "That's the club I belong to." I ask for his name and phone number in case I get into trouble. He gives me all the information and then goes back to work.

The weather really gets nasty later. It's raining and the wind is blowing so hard. It isn't long before my second battery is empty. I'm on a country road. The farms are far apart. I push the ELF, because I can't even pedal it. A car comes out of a driveway toward me, but passes me. Next thing he stops and turns around and asks me if I need help. I ask him if he lives there, pointing to the driveway he came out of. "No," he says, "I just bought a piece of machinery." "Then someone is home there?" I ask.

It's a long way to push the bike and the driveway is long and steep. When I get there, a lady comes out. "Can I help you?" she asks, in a very kind and friendly voice. "Yes, you can. I'm out of power and the batteries are dead. I have a charger and an extension cord." We plug it in and go into her beautiful house. I call Yureks to tell them that I am having trouble. They say they can pick me up with a trailer. I tell them where I am and that I will put the bike by the road so that they can find me.

We go back to visiting. Her mother, who is in her nineties, has come from Germany and had endured some horrific problems. After about an hour, Duane Yurek and another guy come to the door and introduce themselves. I say my goodbyes and we walk down to the bike. Well, the trailer is too short. They have to get someone else. I go back to the house and we visit some more. I tell her that I'm going to be at a Lions meeting that evening and I invite her to come.

An hour later, they come with a bigger trailer. We go right to our meeting. I am very sorry that I don't remember the name of the lady that I visited with. She comes to the meeting and so does her husband after he gets home from work. He is interesting to talk to. He is from New Zealand, I think.

After the meeting, I go home with Duane and Lynn Yurek.

Wednesday, May 20, 2015 – Still in Silver Lake on the way to Hutchinson.

In the morning Duane and Lynn take some pictures. Then we go into the bar/restaurant and visit. The two show me the bike trail, which is nice, because I would have never found it.

On my way to Hutchinson, I have only ten miles to go. I stop off the bike trail in a little town. I ask a lady on the street if there is a coffee shop in town. "Oh yes," she said, "right over there on the corner." I go over there. It's new and quaint. I plug my phone in because the battery is running low. I visit a little with the lady in the coffee shop. They opened only two months ago. After a while, her husband comes. He looked at my bike. I tell him something has been rubbing on the back tire. He says he worked at Erik's Bike Shop and that he will take a look at it. "Funny," I said, "Erik's Bike Shop in Rochester worked on it quite a bit." He goes across the street and gets his tools. He hoists the back of the bike onto some milk crates. He loosens some bolts and nuts and I-don't-know-what-all.

I am very lucky. I could not have gone much longer the way it was.

I ask which road to take toward Hutchinson. They tell me, but I take a wrong turn. That is normal for me. When someone says, take a right, I go left. When I tell people that I have no sense of direction and I have trouble with left and right, they laugh and say, "and you're doing what?" I always get where I want to go… after I go out of my way.

I finally get to Hutchinson. The Hutchinson Lions club invited me a long time ago. They had heard of me at the last Lions Mid-winter Convention. They reserved a room for me at the AmericInn. The Hutchinson Lions club has a meeting and I give a talk about my journey. It's all very, very nice. After the meeting, we go to my ELF. People ride the bike and everyone has a good time. One of the ladies' father rides the bike. The daughter says, "That bike would be great for him; they just took his driver's license away from him."

Thursday, May 21, 2015 – Hutchinson, Minnesota to Kimball, Minnesota

I always get up very early, like four or five in the morning. I suppose that comes from working nights most of my life. This morning as I get my bike ready, a young girl comes and talks to me. She is a 3M Engineer and had been in Singapore. All the wonderful people I meet are all interested in the ELF.

I am on my way to Kimball. It is about a forty mile stretch. Somewhere along the way I lost my Lions flag. I looked for an hour along the ditches of the country road, but I never did find it. This made me without the Lions flag until I got back to Rochester. When I get to the city of Kimball, Minnesota I stop at a very nice restaurant. When I get in the restaurant, there is a commotion right away about that contraption I was riding. I order a hamburger. I can eat only half of it, it is sooo big. Then I call Lion District Governor Duane and Marilyn Finger. Duane answers. "Hi Duane, this is Hanna, I'm in Kimball at the restaurant having a hamburger I have half of it left, can you come and help me eat it?" He says, "Sure, I'll be right there, and then you can follow me home."

I hadn't met him before, but it seems like I have known him forever. He comes and eats the half of the hamburger. I think this is the most excitement that restaurant has seen for quite some time.

The manager will not give me the ticket for my food. "It's on the house," he says.

We go out to my ELF. Three or four people are standing around my bike. One of the guys throws a hundred dollar bill on the seat of my bike and says, "I had a good year, do with it what you want."

Since part of my journey is to do fundraising for Leader Dogs for the Blind, I decide to give the hundred dollars to Duane to write a check to send to Leader Dogs for me.

After all that, we go to the grade school just before it is time for them to go home. We push the bike into the gym. The teachers have all of the kids come in and sit on the bleachers. I tell them a little bit about my journey and there is still a little time left. I say, "One of you can ride the

ELF." Everyone raises their hand except one little girl on the end of the bottom bench. She looks kind of shy. I walk over to her and ask, "Would you like to ride the bike?" She gets up and walks over to the bike and crawls into it. I give her instructions for the controls and how to use the bike's pedals and she takes off in the gym. The other kids all say, "She is so lucky!"

After that, Duane escorts me to his house in the country. In the evening, we go to a Zone meeting where the District Governor is invited and about ten clubs or so take part in it, depending on how large the zone is. Every year they vote for a new District Governor. He has a lot of work to visit all the clubs in his District. That group of people collected 402 dollars for Leader Dogs. What a day! Then we go back to the farm and get a good night's sleep.

Friday, May 22, 2015 – Kimball, Minnesota to Paynesville, Minnesota

I am leaving early in the morning for Paynesville, Minnesota to stay at Lion Patricia Koski's. On the way there, I stop at a Lions' park (dedicated or sponsored by Lions) on quite a large hill. No one is there. It's a nice park. They have a bathroom facility and drinking fountain. I need a little rest. I pull my sleeping bag out. I leave it rolled up, set it against my bike and sit on it and lean my head on the ELF. It is really quite comfortable. I actually doze off a little bit, until a lady comes driving up the hill.

She tells me, "I was visiting my mother in the house down below." She pointed to the house. She saw me drive by and thought; 'if she's still there when I leave, I'll go up there and see what that thing is she's riding.' I tell her what I'm doing; among other things that I am promoting Lions, Leader Dogs for the Blind and Toastmasters. I tell her what Toastmasters has done for me. At the end she pulls out a twenty dollar bill and says, "You can do with it what you like." I say that, if it's ok with her, I will give it to Leader Dogs, but a check would be better. Leader Dogs has sent me printed envelopes with a stamp: "Hanna's Ride." Before I know it, she has her check book out and writes a check for a hundred dollars. She says, "I'll meet you in Hawick, Minnesota . I'll introduce you to some people." After she mails the letter, she introduces me to a lot of people. She was a business person in that town. No wonder she knows so many people. After that, I go on my way to Paynesville.

It's evening when I get there. Pat has a little Pomeranian service dog. It's not for her, but rather for the nursing home. They call her when someone gets out of control, then she goes there with the dog and the dog calms them down. It's amazing what that little dog can do.

Saturday, May 23, 2015

I am on my way to Miltona. There is no bar or anything. It's a very lonely stretch. I stop between nothing and nothing. I am glad to have some potato wedges that are not too green yet and some chocolate from a Leader Dogs fundraiser.

I AM STILL HAVING THE TIME OF MY LIFE!!!!!!!!!!!!!!!!!!!!!

It's about three in the afternoon when I arrive in Miltona, Minnesota at Lion Bonnie and Dan Shay's. Bonnie is working in the garden when I arrive. I briefly explained to Bonnie how I got her name; I got it from her brother, Ted Steidl. I explained previously, when I was at Anna Wickenhauser's house, how I met Ted.

We go into their beautiful, very new, big house. Bonnie is the oldest of a big family. She never wanted children of her own. She says she had enough nieces and nephews. The kitchen is very big, arranged for lots of company. She has a very long and wide island with the stove and sink and everything right in that island. There are chairs on the opposite side. Whenever people come, she can visit with them while she is working; cooking, doing dishes, or whatever else.

Sunday, May 24, 2015

People come and go. I get to meet lots of the Shay's friends and relatives.

Monday, May 25, 2015 – Memorial Day (Miltona, Minnesota)

Bonnie doesn't want me to leave on Memorial Day, but I am supposed to be going to Park Rapids. It's a little far for one day for me. Bonnie insists on trailering me and the ELF there tomorrow.

Tuesday, May 26, 2015

In the morning, I go to the grade school with the bike. We go outside, and the teachers ride the ELF. The kids get to watch. It's all a lot of fun. After that I go to the newspaper and we do an interview. I don't know how often I am going to say this, but it is all so amazingly great. People are all so amazingly great. It can't get any better.

As soon as Bonnie gets home from work, we load the ELF onto the trailer. It takes some doing to make it fit, but we get it to work. We head to Park Rapids, where I will stay with Flo and Carter Hedeen. It's a pretty long ride. We do a lot of visiting on the way. I tell Bonnie how I know the Hedeens…

 The Hedeens and Tommy

I was born in 1942, in the middle of World War II. It takes a country a long time to recover from a war. I would hear about children losing their parents and ending up in an orphanage. I would hear about people being in refugee camps with babies and no food. I thought it was so horrible. That was when I decided, as a child, that I didn't ever want to get married and I never wanted to have children because I didn't think that I could handle that atrocity. Well, life goes a very different direction than one thinks when one is a child, doesn't it? But I never forgot that idea.

I got married, and we had Karl, and three years later Andrea was born. After a few years I inquired about an orphanage. I called the social service in Rochester where we lived at that time, and asked where there was an orphanage. They said, "We don't have any orphanages, but we always look for foster parents." Well, needless to say, that's how we got started as foster parents.

For many years I took babies that were up for adoption.

Janelle was 11 years old when she came. They had called me about her. I said no, because I thought at eleven they are usually pretty messed up. They were desperate. I finally agreed to take her. She is now 58 years old

and I can't imagine my life without her. She never gave me a minute's problem. I always say, "She's like my right arm."

The last baby I got was Tommy. Tommy was born in 1971, with a liver disease called alpha one antitrypsin deficiency. The doctors didn't expect him to live to be a year old. He was not adoptable. He lived to be one then two and three, four, five and six. The social workers always stayed in touch. They always said that we were permanent foster parents. Then they switched social workers on me. This one had different ideas. She said every child should have a chance to be adopted but you have first chance. Unfortunately, we were getting a divorce and the fewer children are involved the better. That's how Flo and Carter Hedeen came into our lives. They adopted Tommy. They gave him a good home. Carter was a medical doctor and had all the means to take care of Tommy's health problems.

Flo and Carter greeted and welcomed us with open arms. They are lovely people. Bonnie visited for a little while then went home.

Wednesday, May 27, 2015 – Park Rapids, Minnesota

I definitely have a good time with the Hedeens. They're just like family. They take me to downtown Park Rapids. Some of the Lions came, even though Flo and Carter are not members. Different people ride the ELF around and around. Everyone has a good time.

Thursday, May 28, 2015

Good morning America!!!! I feel just so great. I feel that way every morning. Today I am going to Staples, Minnesota. Flo and Carter ride along on their bikes to help me out of town. That's great. We bid farewell and I go on my way, about 50 miles to Staples, where a relative of Lori Bates (Remember, I was her nanny?) lives. I can stay overnight at their house.

Tommy – began his life in Chatfield with a rare liver disease

Submitted by
Andrea Elshoff Mueller

Tommy (Thomas James - "TJ") began his life as a foster child to my mom, Hanna Elshoff, and my dad. Born with a rare liver disease, Alphal-Aantitrypsin Deficiency, she was told he wouldn't live to be 2 years old. At age 6 no one could tell this energetic and charismatic child had a bad liver. Local people still ask me about my former foster brother who, with any chance, would climb on their laps to tell them a story.

Tommy
(Thomas James - "TJ")

Since he was still alive at age 6 and doing well, and my mom's marriage was not, she decided he deserved a chance to be adopted. The terrific parents from Park Rapids, Minn., who adopted him were told he wouldn't live to be 12. They generously took him in and provided him love and opportunity. Our families have kept in touch throughout the years.

TJ remained a very energetic, hyperactive child – to put it lightly. He was a strong doer on the "doer vs. thinker" spectrum. As his parents said, "He was a handful." He loved tractors, cars, trucks and driving.

In high school, he was an avid athlete competing in hockey, track, cross-country, football (as manager) and golf. He was also active in 4-H showing chickens and many other exhibits at the county fair, and attending the State Fair in Share-the-Fun. In college he served as team manager of the hockey team.

Along with his family, he enjoyed the outdoors, camping and canoeing in the BWCAW and Minnesota state parks, including on the North Shore.

His "always-on-the-go" personality drew him to driving truck after college.

Just one year ago, defying statistics and still alive at age 35, he married Mickey and, more than willingly, became a father figure to her two charming boys, then ages 5 and 8.

Still in their honeymoon stage, six months after their wedding, his body started showing signs of stress from a poor functioning liver. He visited Mayo Clinic many times for fluid in the lungs and other fluid retention issues. Around Thanksgiving last year he collapsed at work while on a truck route in Iowa. He got sent to the transplant floor at Rochester's Methodist Hospital (Mayo Clinic). From then on he was in and out of the hospital, critically ill and in need of a new liver.

He was put on the waiting list for a liver and his goal was to stay alive and well enough so when a liver became available he would be ready for the operation. In early April, due to his severity, he was put in the top group of individuals needing a liver ASAP. Two times there were false starts on possible livers. Two times his immediate family rushed down from the Minneapolis area in hope of a transplant. The donated liver has to be healthy and match the recipient in a few ways, and they didn't.

Then, on a Monday this April I got a call from him, he asked me if I could come to the hospital to be with him because there was another possible liver. He said he didn't want his wife and mom to drive all the way down if it was a false alarm. I was close by in Chatfield and could get there in 30 minutes to be with him. I got there at 5:30 p.m. and we waited to hear if the liver was a match – if so, it would be coming from two states away. If the transplant were to happen he would again go through the whole standard prep for operation and he'd call his wife and mom to come down. As we waited, he and I talked and he seemed to be in reasonable good condition considering the circumstances. He was weak and the whites of his eyes were not white, but yellow from his failing liver. He needed a liver or he would die.

At about 11:15 p.m. the hospital staff rushed into the room

Mickey and Thomas 'T.J.' Hedeen on their wedding day, April 28, 2007.

and said, "Let's go man." It was a little confusing, but the liver was already in the building and it was a perfect match. He had to be rushed to surgery. He made a quick call to his wife to have her and his mom come down. I went with him as far as I could. We prayed for everything to go well. I waited at the hospital until his wife and mom got there and then I went home.

In the morning I was nervous. I knew it was a six hour operation. I tried calling the hospital, but couldn't get any information. Finally, at 8:30 a.m. I got a call from his mom. "We lost TJ. His heart stopped and they couldn't restart it."

This takes your breath away. It's heartbreaking, especially for his mom, his sweet wife, Mickey, and her two boys who loved him so much. It's a void, a hole, a loss. How can I make sense of this? Statistically the chance of death during the operation is quite low. The Mayo Transplant Team is one of the best in the world and they did all they could to save his life. The biggest risk is having the body reject the organ after the operation. He made it this far, he was 36. Why now did he die? Why was I the last one to be with him – to hear his last conversations?

I was the last one though, as wrong as that seems to me. Writing this story is one of the ways I deal with it. There's a great need of organ donation. He had to wait until he was at the brink of death before getting a liver. Maybe if he would have gotten one sooner his body would not have been so compromised and maybe he would have survived.

One person can save up to eight lives through organ donation and help 50 others through tissue donation. Almost 100,000 people in this country are waiting for an organ and about 20,000 to 25,000 receive one each year. Some 97 percent of Minnesotans surveyed are willing to be donors, and 40 percent of this state's population have taken the steps to make sure their wishes are understood.

If you are willing to help others through organ and tissue donation it is important to discuss this with your family. Donation can be designated on your driver's license by checking the donation box on the application form. Minnesota residents can register to be a donor on-line at www.DonateLifeMN.org. Residents of all other states can go to www.DonateLife.net. Most questions about donating can be answered from the Web site www.life-source.org.

Besides realizing the need of organ and tissue donation, I took away a few other lessons including the importance of generous love and caring of one another. On the last day of TJ's life, I witnessed his generous love he had for all. Even though I hadn't seen him much during the latter part of his life, he still loved me like a sister and I witnessed his deep love for his family. One more thing; let's take better care of ourselves, if not for ourselves, then for the ones who love us. A loss of a family member is devastating and crushing, especially for children. We can all take steps to live a healthier and happier life.

Chatfield residents Lowell and Betty Wooner with Tommy.

Friday, May 29, 2015

Lori's dad, Bill Bates, has a doctor's appointment in Staples this morning. After his appointment, he escorts me to Fish Trap Lake, where he lives with his wife, Linda.

The Bates are parents of Lori Bates, who is married to Jon Van Loon. Jon and Lori live in Rochester, MN and are the parents of Caleb and Greta Bates Van Loon. I was a nanny for Caleb since he was almost a year old. Three years later came Greta. I stayed with them until they didn't need me anymore. The whole family adopted me as one of them. It's really great.

Bonnie Shay that trailored my bike to Park Rapids

Flo Hadeen that adopted our foster boy, Tommy

Caleb graduates from High School this year. I am invited to that big event. Therefore, I have to be home by June 6th.

My plan was to ride to Rochester for the graduation with Bill and Linda, but they have another granddaughter in Milwaukee that graduates a week after Caleb. They will go to Milwaukee right after Caleb's graduation. They generously offer me their second car to drive to Rochester. I stay a few days on Fish Trap Lake with Bill and Linda.

We go to church on Sunday.

Monday, June 1, 2015

We put the ELF in the garage, and I take off for home with their car. It was kind of weird driving a car again. I made it to Chatfield.

Tuesday, June 2, 2015

Remember, I lost my Lions flag somewhere along the way. I went to Jo Ann's Fabric Store in Rochester and got some gold material for the Lions flag. Then, I went to Stewartville to Claire Mrotek's screenprinting business. I had them print a Lions flag for me again. Then I went to my friend, Jan Antonson, to have her sew the flag to the right size for me, AGAIN.

Saturday, June 6, 2015

Caleb's Graduation!
Congratulations, Caleb!!!

Wednesday, June 10, 2015

Now back to my journey......

I drive the Bates' car back to my ELF at Fish Trap Lake. I have instructions for where the keys are and all of that. I stay there one night. I leave early in the morning. My next destination is Baxter, Minnesota.

Thursday, June 11, 2015

I'm not sure where I am to stay in Baxter. I talk to many people along the way. I take a picture of the Baxter Lions Memorial Gardens. The Lions have a camp and that's where I'm going to stay. They show me which cabin I'm going to use. At this time there aren't any other campers.

I get a phone call from Chatfield that a friend from Germany is visiting. I tell her to take my Saturn and come to see me. She leaves early that day, thinking she would arrive between four or five in the evening. I sit in the park at the camp. This is a beautiful place, with a big lake adjacent. It's very serene.

My friend, Michaela shows up at 9:00 that evening. She doesn't have a phone with her. She didn't have a map with her either. She went very far in the wrong direction. Boy am I glad to see her. She is okay and that's all that matters.

There are two beds in the cabin, along with a table and a chair. That's all; no blankets or pillows. I let Michaela use my sleeping bag. I use my jackets to keep me warm. It all works out okay. We visit for a long time. The only thing is, the smoke alarm keeps going off. It is too late to call anybody. When I first got there the alarm was going off. I told a lady that was working there that the battery probably needed to be replaced. She said she would take care of it. I don't know what went wrong, but we had to do something to shut the thing off. We decide to use the small, wiggly table and chair. Michaela is taller than I am. She climbs up there and I hold the table and chair. It's not a good situation. She takes the battery out. We settle back into our beds. It isn't long before the alarm starts beeping again. There is no way we can get to sleep with that noise. We go through the same maneuver as before. Michaela has to take the whole alarm off.

Finally it's nice and quiet. It's after midnight. All is well until the loons start making all kinds of noise. Michaela has never heard this kind of racket, it's louder than the fire alarm! One of the little chicks must have gotten a little bit too far away from its parents. After about an hour, the noise stops and we finally get some sleep. I hope the Loons will be there in the morning because Michaela has never seen a Loon except on a post card.

Friday, June 12, 2015

In the morning we are invited to a beautiful house for breakfast. We have a great time.

But now comes the time again to say goodbye, especially to Michaela. I hadn't seen her for fifteen years.

How did I meet Michaela?

 How I met Michaela

I had met her in Rochester, in a toy store. I heard two little kids speaking German, and I thought there must be an adult somewhere. I found the mother and started talking to her. The first thing I asked was "Darf ich Du zu Ihnen sagen?" which means, "may I say 'you' to you?" In German we have two words for 'you.' 'Du,' the informal, and 'Sie,' the formal you. It is very complicated. One has to asked permission to say Du. "Certainly," she said. Once we had that out of the way I told her that I was taking care of two little kids about her children's age - Two and a half and five years old. When I started to take care of Caleb he was almost a year old. The father, Jon, asked me to teach him German. I just simply spoke German with him, that is how a little child learns another language.

Michaela's husband was a doctor doing research at the Mayo Clinic for two years.

We became very good friends and so did the children. She and the kids came quite often to Jon Van Loon and Lori Bates' house and spent about half a day. Caleb and her son played so nicely together. It was fun hearing them speaking German. That was what I wanted, for someone else to speak German, not just me. When I spoke German to him, Caleb called it

"Hanna's words." The girls were a little young. They played nicely too. But not like the boys.

It's only four miles from Baxter to Brainerd. I stop at a bike shop. My $250 cycle analyst, which tells me how many miles I rode and what the batteries are doing, had suddenly quit working. 99.9% of that thing is over my head. However, there is a picture of the battery on it, which I watch very closely. It also tells me how many miles I've traveled and how fast I am going. The whole thing just suddenly went dark about a week ago. The bike shop can't figure out how to fix it. I just buy a new speedometer and have them put it on for me. Besides that, there are quite a few loose spokes and other things needidng repair. They take a lot of pictures of my ELF. I am being treated like royalty, AGAIN.

In the afternoon I ride to Aitkin, Minnesota.

On the way to Aitkin, the "ghost" in my bike is back. I'm eight miles away and the power in the battery is suddenly all gone. I switch to the fully charged battery and still no power. I pedal about five miles on my own power and then my juice runs out, too. I'm now three miles from Aitkin. The Lions club has a meeting this evening and they are already waiting for me. I call one of them for a rescue. Three of them show up. I say, laughing, "This bike is like a woman, you have to give it some time to think and it will come to its senses." Of course, they laugh.

We leave the ELF to sit on the side of the road. They take me to the meeting. We have a nice meal. Two guys sneak away to go get the bike. When they return, they tell everyone that everything on the bike was working. The guy that rode it back enjoyed riding it. I sure would like to know what's going on. When the guys walked into the meeting, I was just telling them that before I left on my journey, one of our Past District Governors, Barb Ernster asked me if I had thought about if something would happen to me. I said, "Like kick the bucket?" "Yes," she said. "If I kick the bucket when I am on my ride, (I had thought this all through during the year I planned my journey) the bike would be inherited by the Lions Club where I was at that time, but there would be an obligation to that club: that club had to get the bike to the next club within a month or so." That was my wish. One of the guys that came back, probably the one who rode the bike, comes over to me and jokingly puts his hand around my neck. Lots of laughter!

After the meeting, I go home with somebody, but I don't remember who.

Saturday, June 13, 2015

I stay in McGregor, Minnesota with Tom and Shirley Scotland. They write in my book, "Kiss and Tell." Also, I take a picture on the deck with water on both sides. It is very beautiful!

Sunday, June 14, 2015

I'm on the way to Carlton, MN. It's about 45 miles. I don't remember much about Carlton, except that Mark Othus will pick me up to go to a Lions meeting in another town and take me back to Carlton.

On my way to Carlton, I meet a couple in Tamarack, Minnesota in a very little restaurant. They invite me to stay at their house when they get back to Duluth. I do stay at their house one night.

Monday June 15, 2015

What a beautiful trail I rode to the Buffalo House in Carlton, MN. I took my time. I am at a Lions meeting with Chuck. After a wonderful meal, they had the Installation of Officers by District Governor Mark Osthus. Thank you, Carlton Lions! I have so many people to thank: Marlys and John Estrem and so many more. Most of you are going to Hawaii to the International Convention. Have a great time. I will see some of you in Grand Rapids, Michigan on September 17th at the US-Canada Forum

Tuesday, June 16, 2015

I am in Duluth. I'm staying with Lion Esther. She lives in a cute community in Duluth. I stay with her for two days. I can ride my bike easily from her house to downtown Duluth. However, I have to go up a big, long hill. I make it, but I have to use the power AND pedal. I always like it when people see me. I think as they look out of their cars, they say,

"Look at the old lady; she can really go." Little do they know that I have a power button.

Wednesday, June 17, 2015

Today is the Lions meeting in Duluth. The Lions club has put it in the paper that I am a guest speaker. I go very early. The meeting is at noon in a hotel on the second floor and they want the bike up there. Well, we have to go back to the freight elevator, but we get it up there. It's a great meeting. I get a lot of complements on my speech. It strokes my ego, to say the least. There are quite a few people besides the Lions because of the news article in the Duluth paper.

Thursday, June 18, 2015

I go back downtown to visit a Toastmasters club. I am going on my journey not only to promote the Lions, but also Toastmasters. I give up on that eventually, because I very seldom find somebody that knows something about Toastmasters. I call up a Toastmaster, Jean, in Rochester to get some information in Duluth about a Toastmasters club. They meet on Fridays at noon at such and such a place. She gives me the address. Well, they have changed the location for this Friday. The people in that office building go out of their way to find out where they are meeting today. They give me an address. Consequently, I get there very late. I meet one of the members, who was not informed about the change. Well, it's ok, but not the best. The Lions club did much better for me in Minnesota.

I pedal around downtown Duluth a little bit. I stop at a motorcycle place and get a sticker from them for my bike. Down the road I stop at an intersection. There's a guy sweeping or something like that. He is interested in my bike. I show him how it runs. As we walk around it, I say, "I have this computer. It is called a Cycle Analyst, but it doesn't work anymore. Oh, my gosh! It's working now. I swear there is a ghost in this thing. Well, now I can at least see how far my batteries are down."

I figure it out a long time later that I have to shut the motor off by turning the key off. Then it all works. Like I said before, I'm a slow learner and a late bloomer.

The roads I traveled in Wisconsin

Friday, June 19, 2015

I was advised to cross the St. Louis River on the Oliver Bridge to get into Wisconsin. I got to the Oliver Bridge. It was my kind of bridge. I waited until I didn't see a single car or truck before I started going across it. I met a couple vehicles and that was all.

I am in a little town, Brule, Wisconsin. I decided to stop there. They have a small motel. That's just fine for me. I get a room and right next door is a bar/restaurant. Of course, my ELF creates conversation like

always. I asked about Lions. They were very helpful. They sent me across the highway. There is a lady that belongs to the Lions. She is there by herself. We visited and visited some more. She became like an old friend. Then she said, "Come with me to the bank and see what my dog does at the bank."

The bank teller gave the dog a biscuit before calling the police to report a robber with NO gun. The dog left, only to show up again the next day. He remembered the dog biscuit.

Saturday, June 20, 2015

I went in the morning to the restaurant. A lady was waiting for me. She belonged to a Lions club. She invited me to her house to spend the day and a night. I checked out at the Motel and went with her. I had a wonderful day at her house. Her granddaughter had a great time riding my ELF. I met her son-in-law. Her daughter had died a year ago. We shared lots of stories about someone dying.

Sunday, June 21, 2015

My next destination was Cadott, Wisconsin; 150 miles from Brule. That takes roughly three or four days. I went on small country roads. Beautiful area everywhere. I don't exactly remember what the weather was like. In June, it rains a little more. That didn't bother me. When I travel, I don't get wet, only when I stop. I stayed in small motels along the way. Cadott is where the brother of Past District Governor Clair Mrotek from Stewartville, MN lives. PDG Clair let his brother know that I was coming. His brother is a very loyal Lion. I will stay overnight at their house.

Time to daydream for days, with interruptions when I stop at a restaurant or a bar or gas station. I have lots of time to think about things that happened a long time ago in Germany and wherever else.

 ### Waddack and Janina

My brother told me that, shortly after I was born, my mother was in Verden when trucks of Nazis came in and went into the businesses that were mostly run by Jewish people. The people were loaded onto trucks like cattle, to be never seen again. My brother said that my mother just stood there and cried. I never saw my mother cry. She was kind of tough, but quiet and kind. Lucky for me.

Another thing that happened, I think I was about a year old, the Nazis went into Polish villages that were mostly Jewish and took the people off their farms and out of their houses. They loaded them on trucks like cattle. They brought them to Verden and put them in prison. During the day they put them on farms to work. We had two young people, Waddack and Janina. My father was told that they were not to eat with us; they were to eat in the barn. They were to be treated subhuman. My father did not listen. They ate with us and they were treated like family. I don't know how long they were with us, maybe one or two years.

One day, we were to go to Verden and have our picture taken by a photographer. I think my father had given him some food. My mother could not take us, so she sent Janina to take us to the photographer. I must have been around two years old. He took a picture of us four kids. He wanted to take a picture of just me. I cried, but, when I sat on Janina's lap, I was quiet.

My mother learned quite a bit of Polish. One evening, Waddack had me on his lap. He said in Polish to me "Hanna, I will never see you again."

That night he and Janina escaped.

We didn't know whatever happened to them.

Irmgard, Hans-Heinrich, Hanna,
Manfred

Hanna on Janina's lap.
(the Polish prisoner)

*Poland was the first country freed from Russia. It wasn't long after that
happened in 1989, I was long over here in this country, when my mother
got a letter with the house number 8 on it. Our house number had been
changed to 52 quite a few years ago. Written in poor German, the return
address: Waddack and Janina (I don't remember the last name). They had
gotten married and Waddack wanted verification that he had worked on
the farm for his social security.*

*My brother, Hans-Heinrich went to see them sometime later. They had
some lady translate, but she was more interested in talking about herself. He didn't find out much about Waddack and Janina, except that they
were doing okay. I was always going to go there, but I never made it.*

*All this happened in Gorbachev's time. My opinion was, he was a very
smart man. He had to pretend that he was a real communist, but I don't
think he was. He kept coming to the USA. One time, when he was in
Farmington, Minnesota, I had the TV on. It was snowing outside, and the
TV screen was all snowy. I couldn't see anything. The only thing he said
that I remember, was a Russian proverb: MEASURE A CLOTH SEVEN
TIMES BEFORE YOU CUT IT. I think that is a very good proverb. Think*

about that. If everybody would think about what they are about to say or do, other than a compliment, there would be lot less problems.

One time, a long time ago, when Janelle, my foster daughter, was still in school, she said, "I don't feel good." She didn't care much for school. I thought to myself, you just don't want to go to school. I am, to this day, glad that I only thought that and didn't verbalize it. I said, "Let's take your temperature." She was very sick. Her temperature was 104 degrees.

 ## The Fire

The Allies got rid of Hitler for us, but the rules stayed the same. I learned in school that the Ammies (that's what we called the Americans) thought that every German was a Nazi. My estimate is that about half were brainwashed to the Nazi belief. Nevertheless, the rules were still the same. We had to produce more then we could deliver. Remember, the farms are in the village. They watched us like a hawk. For example, we had two sows. When they farrowed, we had to report to the burgermeister (the mayor) how many piglets were born. We had a basement under the chicken house. No one knew about it. My father would take one piglet and hide it there.

I was five years old, and it was right after Christmas in 1947. This was the coldest winter reported in history. The climate is like that in Washington State. We live close to the North Sea. That affects the climate a lot. Rather than heat the whole house, we only heated two adjoining rooms and lived in those two rooms through the winter.

The water pipes are just a little bit underground. All we had to burn was peat moss. My grandfather, who was killed in WW ll when my father was three years old, had bought a piece of land that had peat moss underground. We had quite a lot of that stuff. My father put some under the pipes to get them to thaw.

It was about eight in the morning. My sister, Irmgard, was helping my father. He left for a few minutes to get some tools. The wind was blowing ferociously. The big barn door blew open. Straw was hanging from the ceiling. It caught on fire from the smoldering peat moss under the pipes.

I still had my night gown on when Irmgard came running, yelling, "The house is on fire."

As you know, the cow barn and the house are connected. We rented the upstairs out to the Bergmann family. Everybody is running. Even though everything is made out of brick, it still burns; especially the straw and the hay. My brother, Manfred, handed me a pigeon that he kept in the house and said, "You take care of the pigeon." Everybody is going crazy. I am walking around with the pigeon. I don't know what to do with it. I go up the already burning steps to Bergmann's. I asked them what to do with the pigeon. "Let it fly, let it fly!" I let it go. It flew right into the flames. I caught it. They wanted me to go down the ladder outside of the window. I was afraid of that. I ran back down the stairs. After that I don't remember much. I walked to Behnke, the neighbors. They were busy cooking food for everybody. I don't know whatever happened to the pigeon.

There were some fatalities. One cow, two calves and a dog all died. After the bricks and mortar got so hot, it all fell into a heap. The upstairs was mostly gone. One bigger room and a couple very small rooms were still somewhat ok. It was now all open to the hayloft.

My sister and I stayed with Tante (aunt) Maria and Uncle Hermann and their three boys. They lived in Verden. They had running water in the city. Irmgard stayed three months and I stayed six months. Manfred stayed with Tante Martha and Uncle Hinni and their two boys in Holtebuettel. They had to take a train to get there. It was too far to walk. My mother and father and Hans-Heinrich stayed at Behnke's, the neighbors. My father couldn't sleep. He blamed himself for what had happened. He sent the men home that were watching the coals at night. My father took over. They didn't have fire trucks. All they had were buckets and a wagon they hauled sewage in. They got buckets of water from the neighbor to the left, Denkers. They had a well without protection around it. The spilled water around the well froze. My father slipped and fell into the well. He hung on

with his fingers. He prayed to GOD, "If you help me stay alive, I will never complain again." He got out and after that he could sleep again.

Six months later, Tante Maria pulled me home in a wagon. I had a big water blister on my heel. I don't know how I got that.

I can still see Irmgard on the rubble of bricks knocking the mortar off. We used every brick to rebuild the barn. The barn was rebuilt quite a bit smaller than the size of the original barn.

Now, getting cement was a problem. At that time, one could not buy anything with money. It was not worth anything. One could only get things in exchange for food. Someone ordered a whole train wagon load of cement, but it was not good quality. It was offered to my father. He shared it with our neighbor or somebody. My father had a pig hidden under the chicken house. He used the pig for trade. My brother, Hans, went to Bremen, where everything was bombed. He found iron trusses. I don't know how he got them home. Maybe with the horse. Hans is not alive anymore, so I can't ask him. I think he was 13 at that time.

My parents were very religious. They believe that GOD helped them. And that was good.

Three years after the war was over, the Americans decided to help Germany rebuild. The people in small towns felt it last. In 1961, when I left, we knew something was going on. Money was being pumped into the economy of Germany from the U.S.. We were still getting care packages now and then. Very few people had a telephone. No one had a refrigerator. We just heard about a television.

 The Popcorn Story

Quite a few years before I left, we got a care package containing some kernels (popcorn). We didn't know what it was. The instructions were to put oil in a frying pan and put some kernels in. It didn't say anything about putting a lid on it or to eat it afterward. We just used it for entertainment.

Whenever we had company we said, "You want to see what we got from America? Food that jumps out of the frying pan." It created a lot of laughter. Then we would sweep it up and throw it out.

We also got peanut butter. We thought it was shoe polish. It wasn't very good at all for that purpose.

THE END OF A LOT OF DAYDREAMING FOR NOW!!!!!!!!!!!!!!!!!!!

Thursday, June 25, 2015

I am in the beautiful city of Cadott, Wisconsin at Clair Mroteks' brother's. I am staying at their house over-night. Clair's brother was a very devoted Lion. I am sorry to say, he is no longer with us. He died from cancer in 2016 sometime after I had been there.

Friday June 26, 2015

The Lions Club had a picnic and invited the whole community. I was the guest of honor. A good time was had by all!

Saturday, June 27, 2015

I am staying one more night. They show me around town. Lots of history in that city.

 Education in Germany

When I was 14 years old. I am done with VOLKSSCHULE (eighth grade). At that time, we were considered to be an adult. Confirmation was a big celebration for the "Landeskirche" (government church), as well as for our church. Everybody, except for us, belonged to the Government Lutheran church. Confirmation was taught in school.

School has changed a little bit. Now they go to school one year longer than when I did. Then they pick a trade. For example, if they want to be a beautician, they get a job at a beauty shop. They sign a contract that the shop

will keep them for three years and let them go to school for one or two days a week. They will get paid a fair wage, vacation and so on. You, as apprentice, will sign the same agreement. After the time is up, the apprentice takes a two-day test. Then they are a Journeyman. That is how it is with all trades. When you are a Journeyman, you can get a job anywhere. You are truly educated in that particular field.

Anyone that wanted to become a doctor, lawyer, teacher, architect or anything else that needed further education, would go to Gymnasium (High School). In the German education system, it is the most advanced of the three systems of German secondary schools. It was decided at fourth grade. They had to go to Verden for a whole week and take tests. My brother, Hans-Heinrich, signed up for it because the teacher thought he was smart enough, but my Dad wouldn't let him go to high school. My dad thought he would get away from the religion. Too bad, his life could have been a lot different. Such is life.

Now, like I told you before, I grew up in the Independent Lutheran church. My father (I hate to say it) was against education, especially for girls. I was to learn to cook and clean and serve a man. He wouldn't let me get a job as an apprentice. I stayed home the first year after eighth grade. Then I got a job a block away from our house in a publishing house as a "gopher." Boy, did my dad watch me. We had the Christmas party at the town's restaurant/bar. They had a nice dance hall with big windows. Dad came on his bike to see if I was dancing. He was dead set against dancing, short hair and all kinds of modern stuff, but we could drink alcohol at fourteen. None of it made sense to me. We were looked upon, in our village, like we look at the Amish or the Mennonites. We went to public school, but, otherwise, we stayed to ourselves, especially on Sundays. I could not even do needlework on Sunday. A lot has changed since I left. Some of it is still the same. I say that is the reason that I wanted to go to another country. The only place my Dad would let me go was to the USA, because he knew that they go to church there. If he only knew.

On Sundays, after church, we would get into a discussion; it says in the Bible that the man is the head of the house. I would say, "That might work for some people, but, just because he is a man does not mean he can make

decisions." Dad would get kind of angry with me and he would say, "The youngest one [meaning me] has to have the last word." Uncle Hannes, his sister Tante Mimi's husband, could not make any kind of decisions. Everybody knew that, even my Dad. I would say, "What about Uncle Hannes?" Dad would not say anything, he would pout because he knew that I was right.

 My First Love

May 1st is a Holiday in Germany. Hitler started that. He wanted to get away from the religious holidays. May first is still today an all-day Holiday. Stores and all business are closed. Many of the different groups get together and go on a day-long bike tour. At 14, I could be with the young adults for the first time (from the church, of course). I had a crush on a boy, Uwe (OO-vay). I went to Confirmation training with him. We had our own in EVANGELISCHEN LUTHERISCHEN FREIKICHE (Evangelical Lutheran Free Church). There were 7 of us; 5 boys and 2 girls. Uwe was always very funny. He was tall and skinny. I made myself look really good for the first of May trip. I had a pleated, plaid skirt and a white blouse and a green corduroy vest on. I looked really good. Was I crushed, when he was holding hands with another girl, Lisa, as they are riding their bikes. That was my first big disappointment in the department of LOVE.

Sunday, June 28, 2015

It is late afternoon. I am hungry. I see a bar/restaurant, called Behind Bars, on the east side of the road. There hadn't been anything for a long time. It was all alone among the fields and the trees. It looked like I wouldn't find any other place to eat anytime in the near future. I stopped and had a hamburger. They gave me a wooden nickel. I could buy a drink with that. On one side it said, "BEHIND BARS." I hung on to that wooden nickel for a very long time. I don't know where I lost it.

Of course, you guessed it, the ELF caused commotion again.

When I was ready to leave, I asked about a motel. They told me there is a nice motel next to a Veterans' Memorial Garden at the end of the road. It's about 6 or 7 miles away. I took off. I stopped at the motel, but they were filled for the night. They told me about a motel down the road in the town of Greenwood. I went down a long hill. I got to the motel; they were full. I had them call the next town; they were full also. I asked if there was a campground. There was one back up the hill and then five or so miles more. I started going and, once I started to go up the hill, my second battery was empty. I had to push that bike up the long hill. The bike pushes easy, but I have to keep one hand on the handlebar and the other arm around the back of the bike. Well, anyway, it is not so easy. I swore they were adding onto the hill. It kept getting longer and longer. I finally got to where it was level and I could pedal the bike. I stopped at the first house to ask how much further it was to the campground. No one answered. Then I went to the next house and the lady, her name was Betty, answered the door. I asked where the campground was. She said about six miles. I saw that they had a big yard, "Do you suppose I could put my tent in your yard?" I am getting pretty tired and my batteries are dead. About then her husband came and said, "We have that camper sitting right out there; she can sleep in there". Betty told me that she had seen me go by earlier and was wondering what that thing was I was riding, and then I ended up staying at her house.

There was going to be a celebration at the Veterans' Memorial across the highway the next day. Betty asked me stay another night and I did.

Thank you so, so much, Betty. That was so wonderful. I just can't thank you enough.

Everything is just too incredible.

Monday June 29, 2015

I am heading for Appleton, Wisconsin. It is evening. I check into the first motel I see. It looks like one of the better ones I have stayed in and it cost only $55.00, no more than the less fancy ones. I guess because it is a Monday and they are not busy. I get my stuff and my sleeping bag.

I always sleep in my sleeping bag. I put it on top of the bed. I use my small lap blanket filled with feathers as a pillow. I started that at the very beginning of my journey. I use that system wherever I go. As far as I am concerned, they don't have to change the sheets. They say they do; that is their problem. When there is a couch in the room, I sleep on the couch. I love sleeping on a couch. At home I sleep on a couch.

I get up early; about four in the morning. In a motel, I usually visit with the night person. Since I worked the overnight shift most of my life, I can understand what they go through. Other times, I work on my Face-book page, or try to. Also, many times I am trying to figure out where I want to go, the route I am going to take and so on and so forth. This morning, at about at 8 A.M., the day shift came. A little bit older lady came in. I asked her if she happened to know a Lion. To my surprise, she did. He lived only a couple of blocks away from the motel. He was President of the club for the year. She said she would call him as soon as she had time. Then she found out that I didn't have a plan. Oh boy, did she get upset, in sort of a caring way.

The Lions President came by after a while and sent me to an area called Chain of Lakes where his parents and his brother have cabins. He gave me a shortcut to get there. It was quite easy. He told me that he would come later. He had some work to do.

I took off. Naturally, I got lost. I ended up in a somewhat deserted area with a big gas station at a big intersection where there is entrance to an Interstate Highway. I parked my ELF. Many people stopped to ask about the ELF and, once again, it takes a while just to get into the gas station. People just walking by wanted to know about the contraption. I am always glad to answer questions.

A lady walked into the gas station just ahead of me. I said to her," Excuse me, ma'am, are you from this area?" "No, I am from Minneapolis, Minnesota, but my parents live on the Chain of Lakes. I know this area pretty well." I showed her the address where I wanted to go. She told me how to get there and then she said, "I am going to my parents. They live a few miles down that road. Come and see us if you don't have anywhere else to go." She gave me her phone number. I thanked her and went on my way.

I found a bunch of cabins. One of them was the Lions President's brother's. The other was where their parents lived. Across from the cabins was a big grassy field. Lots of kids had gathered around the ELF. Everybody rode the ELF. They all had a great time. They were all delightful people. The brother gave us a long ride in a very large pontoon boat; from one end of the big lake to the other. When that was all done, the dad took me into their house and showed me the wood carvings he had made. He wanted me to pick out something I liked. I picked out a cute little dog that sticks to a refrigerator. After all that, I thought it was time for me to leave. I bid them all farewell.

A gift from the people I spent the afternoon with; it's just a little memento for my refrigerator

I rode a little way and then I stopped and called the lady that had given me her phone number. She welcomed me and gave me directions to her parents' house. Her father was sitting outside by the lake. I walked over and visited with him. His daughter came out and so did his wife. It didn't take me long to figure out that the father was suffering a little bit from dementia. They invited me to stay overnight. I gladly accepted. In fact, they invited me to stay through the 4th of July Holiday, and I did.

Children and grandchildren came. The house was big, but it was full. It was a lot of fun. I felt like I belonged to them.

Saturday, July 4, 2015

What a day! In the evening, the fireworks over the water were out of this world. It was all just so wonderful. How did I end up with these people?

Sunday, July 5, 2015

This was, so far, the hardest goodbye. We took a quick picture and I pedal off toward Appleton. I stopped in Appleton at a coffee shop. Someone came running in and wanted to know if he could interview me for the paper. I was always game for any kind of interview.

Later, as I peddled around town, I thought to myself, "Rich gave me a tent and I haven't used it. I wonder if there is a campground around." I asked someone and they pointed to lots of trees. "It's not far from here; you just go right and then left and straight ahead." Well, it doesn't take me long to get lost. I rode and I rode and I asked and I asked again and again. It was evening when I finally found it. It was a State Park with a very nice office. I signed up for two nights. They gave me a number. I had to ride a way to find my assigned spot. It was dark. Across from my spot was a big tent with a lot of people. They invited me to join their party. I had no idea how to set up the tent, so I asked if someone could help me. Three young guys jumped up to put up the tent. I said that they could ride the bike. They all got a turn. All the ELF's lights were on. It looked nice in the dark and they all enjoyed that tremendously. When I returned to my spot, those boys had everything ready; the air mattress was pumped up, my sleeping bag was rolled out, everything was ready, all I had to do was crawl in.

7/7/15

Hanna,

I just wanted to say goodbye. My shift is done for the day and won't be back again until Friday. You are an amazing person and I'm grateful for the short time we spent together talking. I'll be thinking of you and saying prayers for a safe adventure. I'll also be following you on Facebook.

Wanted to give you something to remember your stay in the park.

Safe Travels!

Ranger Chad Ewing

Monday, July 6, 2015

I rode around the park and then went to town. I found a restaurant and got interviewed again. Then I rode around a huge lake. When I got back to my tent, I had company in my tent, two squirrels and a bunch of chipmunks. I had a heck of a time getting them out of there. They cleaned out my peanut butter. They ate all my crackers. They ate everything. I had to go to the gas station and get more food. When I got back from shopping, I found a very nice note and a gift from Ranger Chad.

I posted the following response on my Facebook page: Thank you, Ranger Chad for the work you do. Thank you for the wonderful note you left along with the shirt. I will treasure it. Also thanks for finding the newspaper with the article that was written about my journey.

All that was so kind of you. Only one thing, can you make the chipmunks and squirrels behave a little better? They decided to have a party in my little tent. And I mean a party. The raccoons lack education also. I saw a couple of pieces of litter near the ELF. There were glass cleaner wipes and an empty zip lock bag out of the back pocket of my bike. If you could have some kind of meeting with the raccoons and explain to them, that is not very good behavior. Oh, life is not perfect. All of you that keep these parks going, thank you. I'm glad I had my first camping experience at High Cliff State Park in Sherwood Wisconsin. Peace, Love and Hope to All.

Tuesday, July 7, 2015

I am on my way to Kiel, Wisconsin. I had made connections with a Lion in Kiel. (I had forgotten his and his wife's names. After searching almost three years, in my hundreds of papers and notes, I found their names; Lloyd and Linda Borneman. These two did so much for me and I could not find them anywhere.)

After Lloyd got my very first letter, he called LEADER DOG FOR THE BLIND in Rochester Michigan. He didn't think that I was for real; probably, because of my age, he didn't think I could be doing something like that. When I checked out ok, he sent me an email and invited me to Kiel, Wisconsin. I emailed him back and thanked him for the invitation. I let him know approximately what day I would be there.

How I met Jurgen

I have a friend that lives in Kiel, Germany. He was going to come to Kiel, Wisconsin to see me. He never made it. This is how I met Jurgen Hansen, my German friend from Kiel, and how he came to my house in Chatfield, MN.

Janelle, whom I raised as a foster child since she was eleven, got married in April of 1982. She and Kevin bought a mobile home and put it on the farm close to my house. Janelle was working at Tuohy Furniture in Chatfield. She became friends with a lady, Sharon, who lived in Chatfield. One day, Sharon called me saying, "There are a couple of guys here from Tennessee. They are buying wheels from Mobile Homes. They picked up a hitchhiker who is touring the USA. He is from Germany. Shall I send them over there so he can visit with you?" I said, "Sure. Send them over."

They came in a short while. The first one that got out of the car looked very scruffy. I thought to myself: I hope that is not the German guy. He had very long hair, a beard and all kinds of hair on his face. Then came the other two. They looked a little better, but not much. Well, the one with all the hair on his face was from Kiel, Germany. I had made coffee and we had cake and cookies. We visited for about an hour and they left. To be polite, I said to Jurgen, thinking I'll never see him again, "If you're in the area again, stop by."

A week later, he came walking up the hill with his backpack. He asked if he could put his tent in the pasture for a couple of days. Even though I was a little afraid of him, I said he could sleep in the house. Someone had given me a big German shepherd named Molly. Molly was very protective of me. She was always by my side. I worked nights Monday through Friday in Rochester. During the day, I milked a few cows. It was a Saturday when Jurgen came. I always slept on the couch with Molly beside me.

The first morning, Jurgen got up about 8 A.M. I was done with the milking. He asked if there was anything he could do. He was from a big city and had never been on a farm. I didn't know what to tell him. I was heat-

ing the house with wood. On the side of the house, I had a big wood pile. It was all in disarray. Jurgen said, "You need a roof over that wood pile. My father is a contractor. I have worked on buildings. I can build you a little shed." I had a whole lot of old lumber. He could not build that in two days. That is how it started with Jurgen. He became friends with Jon Van Loon, a bachelor who helped me a lot. I will tell you another day when I daydream about how I met Jon Van Loon. I let Jurgen drive my pickup to Rochester. He met up with Jon and they went to bars or something. Every once in while he would say to me, "I better go pretty soon; I came to see the USA." I told him, "You've seen Chatfield; you've seen the USA."

Thursday, July 9, 2015. Kiel, Wisconsin

When I got to Kiel, I stopped at McDonald's. I didn't get out of the ELF yet when a young mother and her son came running out of McDonald's. "Are we glad to see you. We saw in the paper that you were coming today and my son has a birthday party tomorrow." The boy was probably about 9 years old. I let him ride the ELF. He had a really good time. We went into McDonald's. They finished their meal. I gave them a business card, and then I said that I had to make a phone call. I called Lloyd and Linda Borneman to let them know that I am in Kiel at McDonalds.

It didn't take them long to arrive. We all visited. The lady left with the boy. After a little bit, the lady and boy came back in. She had seen on the back of my business card that I am doing a fundraiser for the Lions LEADER DOG FOR THE BLIND. She gave me some money and the boy gave me a Silver Dollar that his Grandmother had given him. I never got their name.

After that I followed the couple to their house. The next day a special Lion's meeting was held.

I stayed in Kiel three nights.

Sunday, July 12, 2015

In the morning, I am on my way to Milwaukee. I am wearing my hat with LEADER DOG on it when I check into a motel. The guy, who was from India, that checked me in asked if I belonged to a Lions club. His nephew is a Leo (a Lions Club for teens) in India. It is great to hear stories like that. The next morning, I rode my bike to Lake Michigan. It is huge. It reminded me of being on the ocean when I immigrated from Germany.

 Coming to America

In August of 1961, when I was 18 years old, I left the village of Borstel in Germany headed for America. My brothers, Hans-Heinrich and Manfred, drove me to Bremerhaven (about 2 hours north of Verden). About 20 young friends and relatives escorted me to Bremerhaven; they want to make sure I'll leave. (just kidding) I had two big suitcases, made out of cardboard, packed with a variety of things. I didn't have very many clothes. My father could not say goodbye. He went into the field and

worked. My mother did not have a problem with that. We shook hands. We didn't hug. She said, "Write once in a while." We got to Bremerhaven at noon. The ship MS BERLIN was docked and ready to be loaded. Everybody could get on the ship and look around all they wanted for all day until evening. A whole train load, starting in south Germany, of immigrants got loaded onto the ship.

Every visitor off the ship!

Picture this: evening arrives; the sun is setting; the gangplanks are being drawn. They have a military band on the side of the ship playing songs like ADEE DU MEIN LIEB HEIMATLAND (Farewell Dear Homeland) and several other songs on that same order. I don't know why I didn't shed any tears or even come close to tearing up. I was a lot tougher in those days.

I had a cabin with three other women. One of them was going back to the USA. She had her citizenship already. The other lady was going to visit her sister in New Jersey. I don't remember where the third was going. All I remember is that they all stayed on the East coast. When I told them I was going to Iowa, they said, "That is a long, long way." I had no Idea. We didn't visit with each other very much. The only thing I remember vividly; while we were in the middle of the ocean, it was announced that the Berlin Wall had been closed. The one lady that was going to visit her sister in New Jersey was from East Germany. She cried the rest of the trip. I don't know what she ended up doing.

One of the days the weather got bad. I got very seasick. The Captain chased me out of the cabin. I struggled my way out onto the deck, and I laid down on a lounge chair. You see, I don't have a reverse gear. I get so sick, but I can't return anything. I laid there and I thought; if I die now, that's ok. The next day the weather was better.

We spent ten days on the ship, then we arrived in New York.

We did not have to stop at Ellis Island. That had closed six years earlier. They still had to have immigration officers on board. They came on the ship two days before we got to New York. A ship is like a hotel on water. They used a party room for the officers. There were four of them. We had long lines. Each one of us had a big manila envelope that was sealed at the

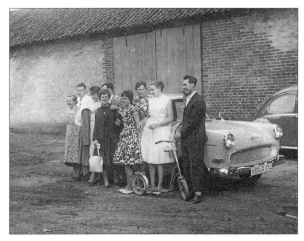

American consulate in Hamburg. (I don't know where the people from south Germany had to go, but I went two times on the train to Hamburg to make the arrangements for my trip to

In front of our shed

America. My sponsors had to write a lot of stuff and disclose how much money they had. It took almost a year to get everything done. In Hamburg, they had asked me a lot of questions about communism.) I was very nervous standing in

Manfred (left); Hans-Heinrich (right)

line waiting to talk to an officer.

Finally, it was my turn. The officer took the seal off the envelope and took everything out.

Friends and relatives

When he got to my chest x-ray, which was a little negative, he looked at it then he looked at me and he looked at it again and looked at me again. Then he handed it to the other guys. They all looked at it then he gave it to me. I still have it. I think he just had fun scaring me.

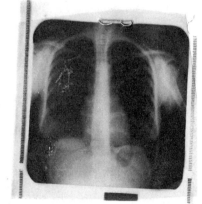

Everything was ok. I got my green card and my chest x-ray.

When we got close to New York, I could see the landscape. The grass was green and the trees were right side up. I thought maybe everything would be upside down on this side of the globe. All the other people were looking at the Statue of Liberty. I think I was the only one that didn't know anything about that.

Friends of my parents, who had immigrated many years ago, picked me up at the ship and took me to their apartment in New York City. I stayed there one night. Then they put me on the train to Minneapolis, Minnesota. I had to change trains in Chicago. I still don't know how I did that; I didn't speak any English.

I arrived in Minneapolis; I don't remember what time; think it was about noon or so. I wrote to my sponsors with my arrival time. I knew what Paul Volker looked like. I had met him in Germany when he looked up his ancestors. I looked around the train station. I didn't see anyone I knew. I saw lockers for my luggage. I fished around in my purse for some change. Some young man came and helped me out and put change in the machine for me. My mind was still in German mode. To me, an 18 year old that had seen very little of Germany, I did not have one smidgen of a clue as to the size of this country. My parents did not have much money. They sent me off with a one-way ticket on the ship to New York, a one-way ticket from New York to Minneapolis, Minnesota on the train and five dollars. I think it was some American money that they must have had lying around. (I don't remember that they only gave me five dollars. Years later, Manfred

came to visit me and gave me $200. I said, "What is that for?" He said, "We feel bad we only gave you five dollars when you left.")

I am at the train station in Minneapolis. I don't know anybody. I knew Volkers had friends in Northfield, MN that they stayed with. I thought Northfield was a little town next to Minneapolis; a little town that I can walk too, like Borstel is to Verden. I go to information. I ask for directions, with the help of my little German/English dictionary. I said, "I am going to walk to Northfield." The guy smiled. He said, "You'd better take the bus." I thought to myself; I understand. In America, people don't walk anywhere; they drive right into their house with the groceries. They take a wheelbarrow to go shopping. I understood why that man told me to take the bus. I go outside the station. I see a bus. That bus must go to Northfield. I waved and he stopped. I go on and I say I don't speak English, I say "Northfield." The guy smiled and said, "Have a seat." He drove and stopped and he drove and stopped many times. I was getting nervous. Finally, he motioned for me to come, I went to him. He wrote something on a piece of paper. He pointed to the direction I was supposed to go. When you don't understand anything, one watches hand gestures. I get to a four-way intersection. Where to go now? I would show a lady or an older man my piece of paper. At every intersection I would go through the same maneuver. I get to an intersection, all I see is a young man, I had no choice but to show him the piece of paper. He pointed to which direction I had to go. I started walking.

I was almost at the point to sit down on the curb and cry. The only thing that kept me from doing exactly that was my brother Hans. At the ship, when they dropped me off, Hans said to me, "You wait until you get to the big America; you'll sit on the street corner and cry and wish your big brother would be there to help you out." That was the only thing that kept me from doing exactly that.

Pretty soon, it felt like someone was following me. I would walk faster and so would he. Next thing, he caught up with me. He started talking to me. It was the same guy I had showed the piece of paper to. I said, kind of abruptly, "I don't speak English." He asked, "German?" I kind of mumbled something. I was irritated. He didn't know any German. I gave him

my dictionary. With it, he explained to me that he wants to help me and show me where I need to go. We walked into this nice big building, which I now know, was the bus station. He bought a bus ticket for me to North-field. We had to wait until 9 P.M. for the bus to leave. I couldn't make any sense of any of what was going on. I was at his mercy. It was about four in the afternoon. I had to wait until nine that evening.

The young man asked, with the dictionary, "Are you hungry?" I said, "No." However, I was very hungry. The people in New York had made sand-wiches for me. They were long gone. I was not going anywhere outside of that building with him. In Germany, they talked how everybody carries a gun in America, and they are not afraid to use it. I wasn't going any-where with that guy. I was staying right in that building. He pointed to a restaurant right in that building. I thought that would be safe. He ordered a glass of milk and a hamburger for me. Which I inhaled.

As I was eating, he talked about the police or something. I thought to my-self; he is in trouble with the police. A couple policemen walked in and they talked to him. Oh my gosh, they already know him, but then they left.

The stranger asked me if I had a phone number. I got my letter out. I had several numbers. "Let's call" he said. We walked over to the phone booth. There were two of them. He went in and then he pointed for me to come in. I thought it was a little small for two people. He explained to me that if he gets them on the phone, I could talk to them." That made sense to me, so I got in with him. Then he closed the door. He dialed and dialed and dialed again. The whole time I thought, I am good with my fingernails, one wrong move and I claw his eyes out. Finally, he said, "Telephone ka-put." We had to use the other phone. But first we had to get out of there. The doors fold to the inside. There wasn't enough room. He had me stoop under the little table the phone sits on so that he could get the door open. A big sigh of relief. At the next phone, I shook my head. He said, "It's too small." That phone worked. He was on it for a long, long time. Finally, he got off and explained, with the dictionary, that they had been at the other train station and are now at the station where I came in.

The young man walked me back to that station. It had gotten dark. In those days, there were a lot of hoodlum's hanging around the railroad sta-

tion. The guy asked one of them for a light for his cigarette. When we got to the station, he talked to the Volkers for a few minutes and then he left. On the way to Northfield, the sponsors said that that young man was a private detective. He was a good-looking young man, I thought to myself. He had written his name and something else on a piece of paper for me. When I got the paper out, it was practically in shreds; I had been that nervous.

To this day, I never thanked that man. I suppose he has died by now.

The next day we went to Iowa to my new home. Paul Volker announced, "Now we are crossing the Iowa border." I started looking for my passport. Paul just kept on driving. I couldn't understand why he didn't stop. Well, of course, I now know what those offices and ramps on the right side of the highway are for; they are for trucks and not for the border-crossing officers. You have never thought about it that way have you

Wednesday, July 15, 2015

I am riding along Lake Michigan. I don't quite know where I am. I went over a big highway. I am in a suburb of Milwaukee. My friend, Jon, back in Rochester doesn't work on Wednesdays. He has a gadget that can tell where my phone is. I call him and he knows that I am lost. His sister-in-law, Lisa, lives somewhere around Milwaukee. He gets me headed in the right direction. I see on a water tower "WHITE FISH BAY." That's where I want to be. Lisa lives only a few blocks away from the water tower. I make a few wrong turns, which is normal for me. Jon, who was still tracking my phone, called me and asked, "Where are you going?"

I stayed overnight at Lisa's house with her family; a very, very nice family. In the evening, I met her husband's parents. Also, very nice.

In the morning, I rode the ELF toward Chicago, Illinois. When I told concerned Lions in Minnesota that I planned on going to Lions headquarters, they had kind of a fit. "We don't like to drive there, and you want to go there on your bike?"

I don't remember much from Milwaukee to Chicago, other than the usual commotion the ELF creates wherever I stop. According to my memory, I stayed in motels on the way to Chicago. It took me four days to get there. I visited along the way and was asked to do several interviews.

Monday, July 20, 2015 - Ilinois

Oak Brook, Illinois; Lions headquarters. I got here last night. I found a hotel within walking distance to the headquarters of LIONS INTERNATIONAL. There are Lions in 206 countries. What I like most about Lions is that they don't have secrets and they don't talk about politics or religion. It doesn't matter what you believe, we are all about service.

Before I started my journey, I contacted them in Oak Brook and told them that I was coming to see them. I was riding a solar powered tricycle. I had names of some people at the office that could help me. What a welcome! I had a great tour; the whole building from top to bottom. I met a lot of people. A beautiful place.

BEAUTIFUL PEOPLE THROUGH THE WHOLE BUILDING!!!!!

I was interviewed for an article that will be placed in the Lions magazine. It appeared in the November 2015 issue.

I stayed three nights at the hotel in Oak Brook. One of the Lions made arrangements for me with a fellow Lion in Indiana. That Lion in Indiana had a gift certificate for a hotel room in his neighborhood, which he was never going to use. I would call him when I got there. He would meet me at the hotel and check me in.

Thursday, July 23, 2015

On my way to Indiana, I am on a bike trail. The trail keeps stopping. Then I ride through a suburb a little stretch until I find the connection with the bike trail again. It is always hard to find the connections. I am in a very old, but very nice housing development. I am riding slowly trying to find the connection for the bike trail. I am riding past a house where there are a couple of men working in the yard. I thought that they didn't notice me. I was past them about a couple of blocks, when I looked in my review mirror. One of the guys was running after me. I stopped the bike. He said, "Would you like to come and have a drink of water and rest for a little bit?" First, I said, "No, I am okay." Then, on second thought, "I think I will." My second battery was running empty; perhaps I could charge it at their place. I had two chargers. One is a slow charger and the other one is a fast charger which so far, had never been used. It was two or three in the afternoon. We plugged the fast charger in and sat on the front steps, visited and drank water.

After while he said, "Why don't you stay here overnight?." After thinking about it, I said, "First, you have to call your wife and get the ok from her; otherwise I will not stay here." He called her and got the okay.

Theirs was a big Victorian house. They slept upstairs or somewhere. I slept downstairs on a big comfortable couch. I always prefer sleeping on a couch. They warned me that the train to Chicago stops early in the morning and picks up people going to Chicago. The train tracks were about 40 feet from the house. They were very close.

Friday, July 24, 2015

I could hear people talking. The train stopped at about six in the morning. Of course, I was long awake. There were lots of people waiting to get on the train. At eight, I started to wrap up my extension cord and put my slow charger away. When I was in the middle of it, the daughter, a teenager, came out to see what I was doing. I asked her, "Would you like to ride the bike?" Her face lit up. "Would that be ok?" "Sure it would be." I said. She certainly enjoyed it. When her father came in, he said, "Let's get our bikes and we can take Hanna to see some really big houses. We have some friends that live not too far from here and we can show her how to get on the right road to Gary, Indiana."

INDIANA

I got to Gary, Indiana at about three in the afternoon. I called my host. He told me that he would be at the hotel. Well, I rode around and around. When I finally found the hotel, he said that he had seen me riding by several times. I got checked in. I stayed there for three nights. The Lion host and his wife took me out for supper that evening. They were incredibly great people.

Saturday, July 25, 2015

Now, I had a big problem; I had left my extension cord and charger in Chicago. My next big, big problem was I didn't get the address, phone number, or name of the people I stayed with. The only thing I had was the daughter's email address. I sent her a message. Then, I got a call from a friend, Brenda, from Rochester, MN. She and her friend, Lance, had been at Lance's parents in Rochester, MI and they would be coming through Gary around noon on Saturday.

When they got there, I told them the dilemma I was in. Lance looked in the computer and I tried to figure out where I had been.

Just as we were looking at the computer, the phone rang. It was the guy where I had stayed. His wife and daughter had gone camping and his daughter just happened to look at her phone and saw the message. She immediately called her dad and told him to call me. He talked to Lance and gave him directions to his house, so Lance and Brenda and I went back to get my extension cord and charger.

What was that; Luck? I would have never found the house where I had stayed; I would still be driving around.

THANKS AGAIN TO BRENDA AND LANCE!!!!!!!!!!!!!!!!!!!!!!!!!

AGAIN, I WONDER, IS IT LUCK OR WHAT?

I question if it's luck or if it's some higher power. Something is guiding me. I don't know what. Something is always keeping me out of harm's way.

Sunday, July 26, 2015

I AM ON MY WAY INTO MICHIGAN

The roads I traveled in Michigan

Sunday, July 26, 2015

I am totally on my own. The first connections I have are in Rochester Hills, Michigan at Leader Dogs for the Blind. Lance told me that his parents invited me to stay at their house, which is not far from the Leader dogs' school.

I looked at a map. I saw a good road and a bike trail I could go on. I do just that. I get into Michigan. Somewhere in Michigan is where the bike trail starts. Don't ask me where or how I figure that out.

Let me tell you, there are always very kind people everywhere. Whenever I leave, there are always a lot of hugs and many times tears. I can't explain it.

At about noon on that trail, I notice a group of people on bikes up ahead of me; about twenty of them. They are all wearing the same matching shirts and pants. They are serious bike riders. They stop for a drink from the water wagon that's waiting for them. Of course, I stop. Everybody wants to talk to me. They don't take much time. As they're leaving, a lady gives me a piece of paper with her name and address and phone number. She says, "You can come to my house in Buchanan if you'd like." I take the paper, put it in my pocket and thank her.

About an hour later, the trail comes to an end. I'm in a town or suburb of a town. I think I'll stay at a motel, if they have one. I stop at a gas station and get information. The attendant directed me to the motel. I don't remember the name of the town.

Monday, July 27, 2015

Monday morning, I get out the piece of paper and look at the map to see where Buchanan is. I find it. It's too far to travel in one day. I ride about 40 miles and stay overnight somewhere.

Tuesday, July 28, 2015

I go another 40 miles today. I stop at a small motel. Practically all of those small motels and gas stations are run by families from India. I always, nonchalantly ask how they like it in this country. I can say that everyone tells me how appreciative they are to live here. The guy at this motel says his brother travels all over the world and says that the U.S. is the best place to live. Then I tell them that I am from Germany and I feel exactly the same way. I manage to hold back the tears until I walk away. Even now, as I am writing this, my emotions get the best of me. I am so, so grateful to ALL the people of the United States. I can't say that often enough. The kindness I find everywhere. Wherever I stop, it gets to me every time. It all turns out to be the way it's supposed to be. Wherever I go, there is a purpose. Some higher power or something is guiding this journey. I just peddle the ELF. As I think about it. My journey started when that bike showed up on my computer screen. With a regular bike, it would not have been the same.

THANK YOU AGAIN, AMERICA

Wednesday, July 29, 2015

Early in the morning, I look at my map. After a long search, I find Buchanan. I call the lady, Fran, that gave me her number. She remembers me and gives me directions to get to their town. When I get there, her husband will meet me and escort me to their house. It's about forty-five miles. I start out on a sort of a bike trail. It's kind of grassy, but I keep going. Then it gets very wet. I decide to go back. I get a good work out. I make it to Buchanan, but I am on the end of my second battery. It's getting low. I call Fran and her husband, Simon, comes and escorts me to their beautiful, large house out in the country.

Fran is a stockbroker at the Chicago Stock Exchange. Normally, they spend weekends on their farm in Buchanan and go back to Chicago on Monday morning. They have a big house there, as well. A farmer lives in the farmhouse in Buchanan and takes care of the farm. They grow hops on that farm. In the last week, the farmer had found a batch of kittens and told Fran about it. Fran is an animal lover and brought the kittens in the house. She decided not to go back to Chicago that week so she could take care of the kittens. If it wasn't for the kittens, she couldn't have invited me to her house.

Thursday, July 30, 2015

Fran calls people for me to meet. She also calls Lions in the town. I ride my bike to town and meet with various people. Fran has to stay home and work. That is totally okay with me.

Fran is an avid rower. In the late afternoon, she goes rowing on the St. Joseph River that goes past their back yard. I sit on the bank and watch her. On her way back, I can hear her breathing from a distance away. She has earned many medals.

Downtown Buchanan is a nice little city. I meet all kinds of people. One of the Lion members tells me that the lions club is going to a camp for handicapped children on Saturday. They will help play games and a lot of other things with the children. They ask me to go along. I accept the invitation. Fran had told me that I can stay as long as I needed to.

Friday, July 31, 2015

I spent the day with Fran and Simon. We walked to the hops field first. The river goes right past their backyard. They built a huge bunker into the hillside where they keep rowboats for the members of the rowing club.

Saturday, August 1, 2015

We left some time in the morning. There was a bunch of us that rode in a van. Other people rode in separate cars. I don't recall which town the camp was in. I remember that I met significant Lions at that camp. They invited me to their houses in Michigan. That was great. I had places to stay.

At the camp, the kids greeted us with songs that they had learned. One of the kids is blind. She must be about eight or nine. After they're done singing, her caregiver tells her to stay there, she will be right back... and I think to myself, that girl has to have total confidence and trust in that caregiver. I suddenly feel so sorry for that little girl. Her caregiver is back in a short time. This little scene has left a lifelong impression on me. I can still see her standing there. She reminded me a lot of Greta (I was her nanny) and how she trusted me, but she could see and everything was what we considered 'normal' with Greta.

The whole day was a great experience.

Sunday, August 2, 2015

Now comes the sad part again; saying goodbye. It seems to get harder and harder. I always have to hurry so that I don't get teary-eyed.

I am heading to Ned and Lou Sutherland's in ("whatchamacallit") Dowagiac, Michigan

It is not very far. I get there at one in the afternoon. Lou told me that a few days ago she read about my bike ride in the newspaper and she was wishing that there was a way to get hold of me. She had just put the paper down and the phone rang. It was District Governor Jeff from the Lions club. Lou and Ned belong to the Lions. Jeff asked Lou if they could take me in.

I just don't know what to think about this journey?????????????? Thanks again to Lou and Ned.

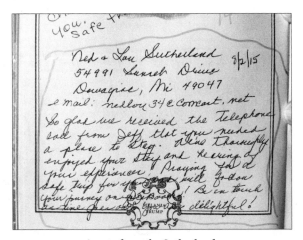

A note from the Sutherlands

Monday, August 3, 2015

I rode my bike to Mendon to District Governor Jeff Meyuiers and his wife's house. Jeff's parents live next door. Both Jeff and his wife went to work in the morning. I spent a good part of the day at Jeff's parents' house.

Jeff works at the nursing home. Jeff had me ride my bike there and give a talk to the residents.

Tuesday, August 4, 2015

Thank goodness for my Facebook page. I am at my new host's, Lion Mary Anne. She lives near Colon, The Capital of Magicians. They even have a cemetery for famous magicians in Colon.

Must find and insert image/picture of cemetery of famous magicians in Colon Michigan

At 6:30 pm, they have a Lions Club meeting in Colon, Michigan. District Governor Jeff Meyuiers is there installing new officers. It was a great meeting.

Lion Mary Anne invites me to stay for the weekend. I am in for a big surprise. They have magicians around the whole town from all over the United States. They give individual shows in restaurants and wherever they can find an audience. In the evening, they put on a show at the

high school. The Lions sponsored that event. It was a good fund raiser for the Lions.

After the third day of riding the ELF to town, I leave it at a Lion family's house, which is close to the high school. That way, I could take it to the high school and leave it there during the day. In the evening I just have a short distance to go in the dark. Otherwise, even though I have all the lights necessary, I don't ride in the dark. I park the bike and ride home with Mary Ann. Mary Ann is very involved in the Lions club; she takes me along to all the Lions events.

Now I have a problem with my ELF; something with the brakes. I show it to different people. No one can figure it out. On Sunday, they have a magic show in the afternoon. After that, I ride the bike back to Mary Anne's house. Marie Anne tells me that she and her brother own a trailer. They can trailer the ELF to Battle Creek, Michigan.

Monday, August 10, 2015

The three of us trailer the ELF to a bike shop in Battle Creek. It's a good thing I let them do that. The mechanic there told us that, if I had continued riding the bike, it would have just stopped somewhere. They have to order parts from Organic Transit and new tires. I don't remember now exactly what was wrong, but I do know I couldn't have gone much farther. I stay with Lion Dianne in Battle Creek until Saturday.

Again, I ask, "Was it luck?"

Thanks, Dianne, for putting up with me and showing me around. Many, many thanks.

FOREVER GRATEFUL TO EVERYONE!!!!!!

Saturday, August 15, 2015

I am on my way to Dexter, Michigan where Connie and Chuck Neese will be my hosts. The Lions have a booth at a festival being held in Dexter. We have planned to meet at the Lions booth.

I take a bike trail, which is very nice, BUT it's barricaded. I look the barricade over. The middle post is sitting in a cement sleeve. I can lift the post out and put it to the side. I do that, push the ELF through, put the post back in and go a few miles and then do it again. I tell you; I get a good work out. Besides that, the bike had been repaired in Battle Creek, but something still isn't right. It seems like it won't shift down, but I have enough battery power.

When I get to Dexter and meet up with Chuck and Connie at the festival, I ask immediately if they have a bike shop in town. They do have one right around the corner. It's about two in the afternoon. I go right over to the bike shop. I tell the mechanic, Jeff, that the bike won't shift. He takes a look at it. Well, he says, "I have to look at it more thoroughly." I tell him that I just had it fixed in Battle Creek and the mechanic's name was John. The company that built the bike is called ORGANIC TRANSIT. I give him all the information. To make a long story short, he reads the instructions, which are very long. He's kind of busy because of the festival, but he wants to fix it.

I leave the bike with him. The next day, Sunday, he takes everything apart. There was one little thing John didn't do because he didn't read the instructions. Jeff gets it fixed. He spent many hours on that thing, but he won't take any money from me. He said, "Kindness begets kindness." It almost makes me cry thinking about it.

I get a sticker for my bike from the bike shop before I leave.

THANK YOU, CONNIE AND CHUCK AND EVERYONE. ALL OF YOU HAVE BEEN SOOOO KIND!

Monday, August 17, 2015

I don't remember where I stop after Dexter, except I remember Novi, Michigan. My collection of friends is getting so big, how I am going to keep track of them. I go to one couple first in Novi. Their cat won't come out from under the bed. They just got the cat. They don't want to put any additional stress on that cat, so they take me to Mary and Manuel Barbosa's, where I stay overnight. I forgot my necklace there. That necklace is the only piece of jewelry I have with me. Greta (I was her nanny) made it for me one year when on vacation with her family.

Wednesday, August 19, 2015

From Novi, I ride my bike to Rochester Hills. This is quite the ride. I remember asking and asking again for directions to Marcia and Stewart's house. They are Lance's parents (He and Brenda helped me get my charger and extension cord back). I'm on some kind of bike trail. It really is something else. I can't put it into words. I go through bushes and someone's yard and I-don't-know-what-all to find the street that will take me to their house. All of a sudden, there it is! Now I can find my way.

Stewart drove me back to Barbosa's to get my necklace.

LEADER DOGS FOR THE BLIND

I am in Rochester Hills for three days. I spend quite a bit of time at Leader Dogs and riding my bike around the city. At Leader Dogs, they invite me for a special meeting. It's a great company to work for. Once a month everyone picks one of their co-workers to honor. That person gets a traveling trophy. I am asked to give a five-minute speech. It is quite the place.

AGAIN, SO MANY PEOPLE TO THANK. 'THANKS' REALLY ISNT ENOUGH, BUT I DON'T KNOW WHAT ELSE I CAN DO.

Monday, August 23, 2015

I am headed for Lennon, Michigan.

When I was in Rochester Hills, I went to a bike shop and had a new inner tube put in one of the front tires. I ride maybe ten miles or so; the tire blows up. It wasn't the right size. They thought it would work, but it didn't. I call BETTER WORLD (like AAA) and tell them my problem. I'm on a somewhat quiet road. It's close to a ritzy area, landscaped beautifully at the entrance. I wait a very long time for a truck to come and pick me up. As I'm waiting, a young couple stops. They were on their way home from work. The guy builds bicycles as a hobby. He's very interested in the ELF. He tells me that he will come to Lennon tomorrow at about noon and fix the tire for me.

The truck finally comes and takes me to my new host in Lennon. When I got to my host's, all the neighbors gathered around. They are all Lions and a really fun and lively group.

The guy came about noon the next day, as promised, to fix the bike. We went to a local bike shop and got the right sized inner tube and he put it in the tire for me. In addition to his kind help, he gave me a tire pump to take along in case I had any more tire trouble.

The next morning, the neighborhood Lions took me to breakfast at the Lennon Café. They are the most entertaining Lions I have run into so far. All of the Lions were good, but this group was unusual.

Wednesday, August 25, 2015

On my way to Frankenmuth

I stop at a gas station to ask for directions and to make sure I took the right turn. Two guys jump out of their pickup. They want to see the ELF. They are kind of "punky" looking. We talk for a while. They're very, very interested in the solar panel. They get back into their pickup and start driving. One of them jumps out and comes running back to me and said, "Wait, wait, there is something I want to give you." I wait and he gave me a picture of his Grandmother. He starts crying and so do I, because he says, "She died a year ago and you look like her. I want you to have that picture and have a safe trip." I don't want to take it, but he insists. I take it and I carry it with me. We hug and we both cry. It's very emotional.

I wrote on my Facebook page:

Eric, if you read this, I will not forget you and your friend, Scott. I wish both of you the very best. Work hard and stay honest. I will treasure the picture of Virginia Baldwin, your grandmother.

Peace, Love and Hope
Hanna

I don't know what it is about this journey?

Frankenmuth, Michigan; a German town I stay in a wonderful campground in Frankenmuth. The Lions have a camper for me to stay in. Frankenmuth is a beautiful, South German town. I can't even describe it. I am afraid you just have to go there and see it. They have a very, very large Christmas store. I would almost think it is the largest in the USA.

The Lions club has a meeting. They have their own building. It's very, very nice.

I travel from Frankenmuth to Essexville; from Essexville to West Branch, Michigan to Mio and then to Grayling. All good roads and terrific people.

Wednesday, September 2, 2015

Mio, Michigan

I don't know what to say about the Lions club in Mio.

(This is to my dear concerned Lions in Minnesota.) One of the Mio Lions had told me that, when I come into town, there will be police waiting for me. Well, three miles before I get into town, there are two police cars waiting for me plus President Lion Randy; *on a two-lane highway!* I'm very embarrassed because all the people on the other side of the two lane road stopped and looked to see what was going on. Then, it starts to rain. When we get into town, it's pouring; I can barely see, but we make it to the motel where the Lions club have a room reserved for me. They have a picnic the next day. I give a talk that evening. The third day, it's still raining. Because of the heavy rain, Lion Randy trailers my bike to Grayling, Michigan. I stay with Lion Clare. I stay there a week;

I don't really remember why. I meet her son, Ray; a delightful young man, who was a chef. He was the cook for a sorority at a large university. He was on vacation at his mother's house and cooked for us. He is an excellent cook. He made croissants for us. Those things are a lot of work but he didn't think so. It sure was fun to eat them. Thanks again, Ray!

Clare worked for the city. She took me along and I met lots of people including policemen.

Wednesday, September 9, 2015

I leave Grayling and am going through a town called Clare. Now, I had heard about this town. A group of policemen had taken over a donut shop that was going to close because the owner had died. I look up that donut shop. They are very busy. I buy a sticker for my bike.

I had parked my bike a block away and walked to the donut shop. When I get back to my bike, a guy with a tandem bike stops to look at the ELF. We get into a conversation, like always. He tells me that his wife had died from cancer. In her honor, he's on a ride that they had planned to do together when she got better. I don't remember where he was from; I think it was Colorado.

Monday, September 14, 2015

I'm in the small town of DeWitt. I just park my bike and walk around. About two blocks away, I find a coffee shop. I go in and have coffee and something; I don't remember now what. There is only one couple in there. They start talking to me. Their name is DeWitt. That's why they came to that town. I don't remember where they came from. About that time, a young lady comes rushing in. She asks, "Are you the one with the solar powered bike?" I say, "Yes."

Her name is Jenna. She had seen me somewhere a couple of weeks ago. Then, she found me on Facebook. She was determined to meet me. I happen to park right in front of her apartment. She had been on a ride and her bike broke down. Her boyfriend went and got her and she had just gotten home. She saw my bike and knew I must be somewhere close by. She started looking and found me in the Coffee Shop.

We left the shop together.

She escorts me, with her car, to the Montessori school in Lansing, MI. She, also, is friends with someone at the TV station. They come and interview me at the school. I met up with Lance's sister, Kristi, at the school. Perhaps you remember, Lance and Brenda helped me retrieve my charger and extension cord. Kristi gave me directions to her house in St. John's, where I will stay with her and her husband, Bruce.

It was fun to see all her livestock; chickens, horses, and all kinds of animals.

Now, on to Grand Rapids and the US-Canada Forum.

Thursday, September 17, 2015

AT THE US-CANADA FORUM

What can I say about the forum? It is always great. I love gatherings, especially the Lions. The speakers are, most of the time, outstanding. Other years, I bought CD's of the speeches at the Forum. This year, I don't see any for sale. Maybe I overlooked them. I still listen to some of those I have purchased in the past. There is so much going on that I can't think of one special thing.

One thing I do remember is, while I'm in Grand Rapids, I get an email from one of my German school friend's (Hannelore) twin granddaughters. The twins came to the USA as AU PAIRs. This granddaughter, Kira, lives with a host family in Huntertown, Indiana. Her twin sister is in Chicago, Illinois. Kira wonders if we could meet someplace. I immediately write back to her and tell her that I will come to where she lives in about 10 – 15 days.

The same day I get a call from Jenna, from back in DeWitt, that she will ride one day with me after the convention is over. I am so excited; I can hardly wait for the time to come.

Sunday, September 20, 2015

This morning, Jenna comes with her boyfriend to Grand Rapids. Jenna is riding a regular bike with me for the day. Her boyfriend is driving a car. They will stay with me until I find a motel in the evening. We drive around quite a bit. I'm afraid I'm going to run out of battery power. It's almost dark when we find a small motel somewhere out by the town of Shelbyville. Now they can go home.

A tough goodbye.

Monday, September 21, 2015

Now, I'm totally on my own again. I don't have to be anywhere any certain time. I don't have any Lions connections left anywhere. Yes, I have the German girl in Indiana. I have never met her. I just know the grandmother, but that's ok. Otherwise, I go wherever fate takes me. The only place I really want to go is to see Jimmy Carter in Plains, Georgia, but that is a long, long way from here, plus there is no date set for our meeting.

For some reason, I stay at that motel near Shelbyville two nights. I think I do laundry somewhere in that town. I made some friends there and they invited me to have supper with them.

Tuesday, September 22, 2015

I drove around town, just looking things over. There was a space of land and then a large building that I thought was an Implement Company or something like that. I pulled in. A lady came out and asked if she could help me. I asked, "Is this a business, like an implement company or something? Is there anybody around?" She said it had been an implement dealer. It is now a place where we put repossessed items.

As she was talking to me, she was walking away to her car. After some rummaging around in her car, she came back with her hand behind her back. I asked her if the road close by would take me South. She said it would and I rode away. I never did find out what she had behind her back. It might have been a gun!

I am not sure which way I want to go. I need to go south. I go on pretty good country roads where there is not much traffic. I been traveling about two hours. I'm in a small town; I don't remember the name now. It looks like a town that would have a motel. I stop at a bank; very nice people; almost like being at home in Chatfield. I am told there is no motel, but they do have very good ice cream at a gas station just a little bit down the road. They make their own ice cream. Of course, they all have to look at my bike before I leave. I wish I knew how to explain how everyone makes me feel all the time. It's incredible.

It's still a little bit early for me to stop riding my bike for the day. I think I'll get some ice cream. I go to the gas station first. Again, what a commotion. Nobody has ever seen a thing like that. Of course, that's not at all unusual for me to hear that. After a while I get my Ice cream, which is very, very good. Then I ask the men that are standing around my bike, if there's a cemetery somewhere. I was going to put my tent up in the cemetery. I've always wanted to do that. One of the men says, " If you have a tent, you can follow me. You can put your tent on my place." I don't ask him how far that is. I think I ride about 10 miles. If I wouldn't have taken that offer, I would have had to go 15 or more miles to find a place with a motel. When we get there, he tells me that I can put the tent anywhere I want to. It's a very huge yard. I find a level spot where I put my tent. I have to figure out how to put that thing up. I get it done. It's still early in the evening. He tells me that there is a festival just a little bit down the road. The Lions usually have a booth. I ride my bike there. The Lions are tending the gate. I make friends with them. Then, I go to see what's going on. I get something to eat. Then my phone rings. I say, " Hello." The man says, "My name is Jim Parker. I am a Lion. Bill Griffith in Chatfield gave me your name and phone number and he had told me what you were doing. You can come to our place and stay overnight." I tell him that I'm in Centerville, Michigan. He says, "That is not very far from Howe, Indiana. It is about 20 miles." "I can be there tomorrow," I say, "Is it okay with your wife?" "Yes, would you like to talk to her?"

I'm so excited, I can hardly breathe. It's funny how everything always works out.

The guy (I forget his name), who so generously let me put my tent on his place, has to go to work early in the morning. I don't know what his situation is. He lives with his daughter and son-in-law, or they live with him. I never did go in the house. It had rained in the night and now it's quite foggy. I just pack up my tent and leave. I ride into town and find County 14. I stop at a restaurant and eat something, and ask if I'm going the right direction to get to Howe, Indiana. I am, so I continue on my way to Indiana.

THE FOLLOWING STORY HAPPENED SOMEWHERE IN MICHIGAN, I DON'T REMEMBER WHERE, BUT I **HAVE** TO TELL YOU ABOUT IT. IT IS ONE OF MY FAVORITE STORIES.

This story starts with Toastmasters, which I have belonged to since about 1982. I found out about it when, on a Sunday morning radio show when I was in the barn milking the cows, Mary Pesch said, "OVERCOME THE FEAR OF SPEAKING; JOIN TOASTMASTERS." I didn't have a pen and paper to write anything down. I was so afraid to even say my name in front of a group of people. I needed help. After two years of searching to find out about Toastmasters, Linda Ottmann, a friend of mine that worked at the Mayo Clinic called me one day and said, "You wanted to know something about Toastmasters? There is something about Toastmasters in the Mayo Clinic newsletter." She gave me a phone number to call and contact Mary Pesch. I called Mary. She told me that Toastmasters meets for one hour at the Episcopalian Church across the street from Mayo Clinic at noon every Wednesday. I joined that club and I have been a member of Toastmasters ever since. It is the best thing I ever did for myself.

Mary quit Toastmasters a long time ago. I never saw her until 10 years ago when I saw her with some friends in the coffee shop at a grocery store. I said, "Hi, Mary. You probably don't remember me, but I have to thank you for telling me about Toastmasters when you were on the radio." She introduced me to her friends. One of her friends was Joyce Gibbs. Joyce is an African American. She is well-known in Rochester.

Joyce Gibbs

They named a grade school after her husband.

Many things have changed since I started Toastmasters. We meet from 7 am until 8 am in the Dan Abrahams building. We walk through a big cafeteria to get to the meeting room. Who do I see there with some friends? Joyce Gibbs. I invited her and her friends to come to visit our Toastmasters club meeting. She said, "I will, some other time."

During the time I was preparing for my journey, the club members had me bring my ELF to a meeting. Joyce saw it and, sometime later, came to our meeting to give a speech about the journey that I was planning.

Mayo Clinic has a children's hospital with a service dog called 'Doctor Jack'. The gift shop at the Mayo Clinic bought a bunch of little brown beanie baby dogs and put a collar on them that said, "Mayo Clinic." Joyce bought one and gave the speech about my journey. She presented the dog to me and said to me, "Since you can't take a real dog with you, I'll give you this."

I had some work done on the ELF at Eric's Bike Shop. I told them that I needed a holder for the dog. They put a cup holder on the right side near the handlebar. I bungee strapped that puppy in there…

Now, on my journey, I am somewhere in Michigan. There is a big construction zone. One side of the traffic has to wait. I am in the middle of 30 or more cars and trucks. After 20 or 30 minutes, we get to go forward. I'm keeping up with the traffic. At the end, I pull over to let the traffic go by. A man in a pickup stops, rolls the window down and says, "Honey, you lost your puppy" and hands me that dog. That dog had never fallen out before and hasn't since. That guy must have stopped the traffic just to get that dog. I wouldn't have stopped to pick up a toy. I never heard a horn beeping or anything.

It still brings me to tears when I think about it.

That's one of my favorite stories to tell about people's kindness in this country.

THAT'S THE AMERICAN WAY!!!!!!!!!!!!!!!!!!!

The roads I traveled in Indiana

Wednesday, September 23, 2015

I still get emotional when I see the state that I am entering. It is just so amazing. One doesn't realize how freely one can travel from one state into another.

I see a farmer's produce stand on a big lawn. I stop the bike and look over the flowers and vegetables. I always like to take something to my new host. When I have the opportunity, I bring flowers or some other stuff. I don't remember what I bought. The farmer came a long way from the barn to talk to me. He said he had seen me on that bike on TV the evening before. He said, "Usually, people who are traveling through Indiana, stay around big cities. They don't come around little towns." I told him, "I stay mostly in rural areas. I like that better."

Thirty minutes later I was at Jim and Sharon's, my new hosts. Like always, they are very nice people. They welcomed me. I told them that I folded my tent up wet. Jim helped me take everything apart and put it out to dry. We had a nice relaxing afternoon and evening.

Jim and Sharon had to explain how they got my number. Jim had a good friend in Chatfield, Minnesota, who happened to know me and my plans for the journey. His name was Bill Griffith. Bill called Jim and told him what I was planning to do and gave him my number.

A farewell breakfast; a compliment from my host

Jim called and asked me to stay with him and his wife, Sharon, when I get to Indiana. He called me just in the nick of time; if he would have called a few days later, I probably would have taken a different route and not been able to stay with them.

The more I travel, that much more I don't understand how everything is working out. Sometimes, when I don't have any connections and I feel just a little bit down, it isn't long when something or other comes along; I have a place to stay.

HERE I GO AGAIN, IS IT LUCK, OR WHAT?

Thursday, September 24, 2015

In the morning, we went to a restaurant with another couple for breakfast. We bid our farewell and I went on my way to Huntertown, to meet up with my German friend's granddaughter. I got there at about four in the afternoon. Kira lives in a very upscale neighborhood. Her host family was leaving on a vacation. They had given Kira a Jeep to drive the whole time she stayed with them.

Friday, September 25, 2015

We picked her twin sister, Anna, up at about noon. On the way home, I had **one big surprise: Kira told us that she goes to church!** (In Germany, very few people go to church other than when they are baptized, married, or buried.) Kira asked if we would like to go along with her? We can go Saturday evening or Sunday morning. We have to go early or there won't be room left. She drove past the church. It said, "Community Church." It was a new, very, very large building. I was amazed that Kira went there. She said her host family went there and she went along. I told her that I would go with her. Anna said that she would go, too. I said that Saturday evening would probably be the best time to go. She was right; that church was full. (Many of you have probably experienced something like that.) The service was definitely for young people. There were some older people there, but mostly young people. It was really quite nice. I guess, if they want the churches to keep going, they have to have more of these services for the young people. They had a good message. I was impressed. Later, on my journey, I found more churches like that. Kira also told us that she goes to Bible Study on Thursday. I thought I wasn't hearing right. Anna's host family doesn't go to church.

Huntertown is like a suburb of Fort Wayne, Indiana. We mostly went shopping in Fort Wayne. I asked Kira and her sister how they liked it in America. They liked it a lot, but they missed the SHWARZBROT (German bread). I said, "Let's go to a supermarket and I'll find you some." In the supermarket, I found the section of imported foods. Those girls were so happy. The store even had cookies from Verden, the city in Germany where the girls and I are from. Kira was so excited. She had worked for FREITAG, the cookie factory that made the cookies. That was fun. We had truly a wonderful l time, even though I was their grandmother's age. The days passed very quickly.

Monday, September 28, 2015

Time to say goodbye. Anna had left Sunday afternoon. We looked at the map on Sunday. Where would I go? We had decided on Marion, Indiana. The girls tried to help me with my monster machine: MY I-PHONE, which I didn't understand at all. They showed me how I could use the GPS; that would be a big, big help.

I took off Monday morning. The weather wasn't the best. I went toward Fort Wayne. I tried to follow the GPS. I felt like I was going in circles. I asked people how to get to Marion. I rode around and around for three hours or more. Suddenly, I was at that church where we had been on Saturday. A young man was mowing the lawn. I stopped him and asked if he could help me with the GPS? He looked at it and set it for me. In the meantime, some people came out of the church to see my bike. We got to talking. A lady, Becky, said, "My mother and sister live in Marion; You can stay with them." She called them up and made arrangements for me. I had ridden probably twenty miles and I was only six miles from where I started. It was too late to go to Marion now. I called Kira and asked if I could stay another night. I had a heck of a time finding my way back. The next day the GPS worked just fine.

Tuesday, September 29, 2015

On my way to Marion, I am on country roads; hardly any farms, just fields.

 My first job in the USA

I am in Fort Dodge, Iowa. I am 18 years old. I don't speak English. Paul Volker, my sponsor, is the only person that knows German. His wife, Clarabelle, is a schoolteacher. She doesn't know any German but is very patient with me. After a few days in Fort Dodge, we went to the state fair in Des Moines, Iowa. Now, that is one of the hardest things to explain. There is nothing like that anywhere in Europe, I think. Now that I am old, I un-

derstand it. When I get company from Germany now, I have them read the book, "Charlotte's Web." That explains it very well.

We are at the state fair. I am overwhelmed. There is so, so much going on. Paul belonged to the Kiwanis Club, a service club similar to the Lions. The Kiwanis had a booth at the fair where they are selling pancakes and sausage. Clarabelle loaded a plate up with pancakes for me. Then she put lots of syrup over the pancakes, which was very kind of her. What she didn't know was that it was all new for me. Most of all, in Germany, we don't eat things so extremely sweet. I just sort of swallowed it down. She thought that I was extremely hungry and she fixed another plate for me. I ate it, but I thought I might get sick. Thank goodness, I didn't.

Paul Volker was an executive for a dairy. He brought samples of ice cream home many times. I had only had ice cream (like poor sherbet) maybe two times in my whole life. I loved that ice cream. I couldn't get enough of it. Clarabelle said "Hanna, don't eat so much ice cream. American boys don't like fat girls." I thought to myself, 'the heck about the boys.'

In order to get my immigration visa, I had to have a job lined up. Paul Volker was friends with Jim Anderson, the administrator at the Lutheran Hospital. Jim had to write a letter to say that I would be working as a housekeeper at the Lutheran Hospital. I went to work after I had been in Fort Dodge three weeks.

I got done cleaning rooms at 2:30 in the afternoon. Once I learned the way home, I walked home. I didn't have anything to do. I was free. In Germany, I always had something to do on the farm. Now I could leisurely walk the 5 or 6 miles (maybe it was less than that). I was used to walking. A nurse would pick me up at 5:30 in the morning to give me a ride. I was soooo tired. I assume it was that I was learning English and all the new surroundings; I just couldn't get enough sleep. I taped an alarm clock to my hand, that helped.

I had gotten my first paycheck. I handed it over to Volkers. I didn't know how much I had to pay for staying at their house. I think I got paid 90 cents an hour. They gave me an allowance; I don't remember how much. I remember that on the way home the next day, with money in my pocket, I stopped at the supermarket. I wanted to buy ice cream. The smallest con-

tainer I could find was a half-gallon. I had to eat that before I got home; you understand why. I would buy that quite often. Then I discovered the Danish rolls. The smallest package was a half dozen. At least they didn't melt. Needless to say, I got a little fleshy.

As long as I am on Fort Dodge stories, I might as well tell you a couple more. The first day at the hospital, the nurse dropped me off with a note containing the name of the person that I had to meet. She told me to go to the second floor. I go to the elevator and said to the people inside, "Second floor." The elevator stopped and there was a 2 written on the sign, but I wanted second floor. I don't know how many times I kept going on the elevator until someone took me by the hand and took me to the lady I was to meet. It was weeks later that I learned that second and two are the same thing. I bet you never thought of it that way.

On the same day, they showed me how to clean the rooms. The first time I went in a room by myself to clean, the patient pointed to a table and said something. All I saw were flowers. I handed her the flowers. She said something very angrily; I have no idea what. I told her, "I don't speak English." She pointed to the table again. There was a table under that table that pulled out from under the top table like a drawer. In it was a toothbrush and toothpaste, and that was what she wanted.

About two months later on a Sunday, Paul and Clarabelle surprised me and came to pick me up. I was late getting off from work. When I got out from work and saw them, I explained why I was late. I said in English "Two cars went boom." Clarabelle laughed and laughed.

My co-workers would tell me something and send me to tell that to another girl. They would always laugh because it never came out the way it was supposed to. They would tell jokes. Everybody would laugh and so would I. Someone would explain the joke to me. Then I would really laugh. On the way home, I thought about it and thought about it. I would finally figure it out and then I would really, really laugh. I would get a lot of miles out of one joke. Humor is the last thing a foreigner learns. One doesn't think about that.

Clarabelle always brought children's books home and had me read them. That was very good for me. When I went to work, I always had a piece of

paper and a pencil in my uniform pocket. In the evening Clarabelle would ask me very slowly and very accentuated, "Hanna, what did you learn today?"

Back to my journey.

Tuesday, September 29, 2015

On my way to Marion, I come upon a town called Roanoke. I stop at a gas station and get something to eat. I go through town. They had one four-way stop. I was on the side of the road. I stopped and so did a pickup beside me with four guys in it. They rolled the window down. The driver hollered something at me, but I wasn't quite sure what. I said, "We have to go." I crossed the highway. The pickup went left. Three blocks down the road, there was that pickup again. The occupants were standing on the road along with people out of a nearby restaurant waving me to stop. I had no choice but to stop. " Come in and eat and drink something" they said. I told them that I had just eaten something at the gas station, but a glass of water would be fine. They gave me a cookie. We visited a while. The driver of the pickup said, "Why don't you stay here for tonight? We have a B&B where you can stay." I called Becky's sister and asked if it would be any trouble if I came tomorrow night. She was totally okay with that. I told her that I was in Roanoke at the JO-SEPH DECUIS restaurant. I stayed overnight in Roanoke.

I found out later who Joseph Decuis was. I think I remember it correctly. Joseph had been a professional baseball player. He had to stop playing because of an injury. He bought a farm and raises WAGYU cattle, which come from Japan. They look like Black Angus, but the meat is better. They raise everything they serve in their restaurants on the farm.

Joe gave me a grand tour of their two restaurants; one was a Bar & Grill and the other, in a larger building, was a fine-dining restaurant. Upstairs in the big restaurant was his office. He had a full-size baseball player up there, among other things. They treated me to one of their steak meals in the Fine Dining Restaurant. It was out of this world.

I think Joe owns most of the town. I stayed overnight in one of their several B&Bs. I don't know what to say about it all. You can look it up on google.

How in the world did I end up in a place like that? I can't explain it.

Wednesday, September 30, 2015

I am back on my ELF. I am going to Marion to Becky's mother and sister's.

I can't grasp what all has happened. I don't have any idea what is ahead of me in Marion.

My new host, Edna

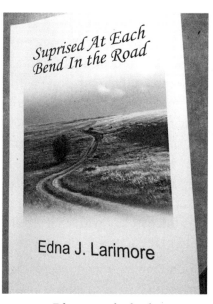

Edna wrote this book,
and she gave me a copy.

It is about 40 miles; an easy day for me; pretty easy roads. I arrived in Marion at about two in the afternoon. I was welcomed by both Betty's mother, Edna and sister, Deb. I spent three nights there. They took me to a Lions meeting. A few houses down is the Indiana Wesleyan University where Edna was a professor. She had two tickets for a special event. Her friend backed out, so she asked me to go. It was super nice rubbing shoulders with all the highly educated people. Here I am with nothing, but I am very happy never-the-less, especially that I am doing what I am doing; riding the ELF.

A very young girl stopped to see my bike. She didn't spend much time at all. She said to give her a call if I needed anything. She gave me her name and number and took off. She lived in Muncie, Indiana. I actually called her and spent one night at her apartment with her black cat.

A young lady and her cat were my hosts.

Tuesday, October 6, 2015

I did not get very far. I stopped in Daleville. I had some kind of noise coming from the front wheel of my bike. They happened to have a small bike shop. The guy looked at it. He found a loose spoke. An old guy that owned the store came and put a new spoke on. I stayed in that town. I stopped at the city hall and asked if they knew a Lion. The clerk did and she gave me the president's number. I went to a restaurant and called him. No answer but I left a message. I never heard from him. I went back to the town hall and asked about a motel. She told me there was one. Then she said, "Just wait a minute." She made a phone call and she said, "You can come home with me."

I stayed there three nights. They had a fall festival in Daleville. They requested that the ELF be there. It draws a lot of attention. On Saturday, I got a call from the TV station out of Indianapolis. They wondered where I was. They asked if they could meet me on Sunday morning and interview me. "That's okay with me," I said. I was always ready for an interview.

Sunday, October 11, 2015

The interview went great. I didn't watch it on TV. I went on my way right after the interview. I don't remember where I stayed, probably in some motel. As I'm riding along through a small town, I pass a lady who is getting her newspaper out of the box. As I rode by, she talked to me. I stopped. She asked me into her house. She was lonely. Her husband had just died. I visited with her for about an hour. I continued my journey. I stopped at an "everything" store. I visited for a bit. Another lady came in and listened to my story. She knew someone that been in WW II. She was about to go home. I followed her. She escorted me to the Hidden Paradise Campground in St. Paul, Indiana. I got a spot there for my tent. The lady's friend, the WW II veteran, came the next day. I have a heck of a time containing my emotions when I talk or listen to a WW II veteran or any kind of soldier. I am very grateful to all the service people.

It wasn't long after Frank Smith, the veteran, left that two young ladies showed up. They wanted to interview me. They had bought a radio station and they also farmed; very interesting people.

I stayed at the campground three nights; one night in my tent and the other two nights in a cabin. The toilets were outside. Whenever I used the toilets, I left the cabin door unlocked. For some reason, the last night I was there, I locked the door. When I got back to the cabin, the door was locked and the key was inside. It was about three in the morning. There was a swing set outside. I still had my jackets in my bike. I got them out to use for a cushion on the swing. I got quite comfortable on the swing set and actually dozed off for about an hour. I got kind of motion sick. I got up and walked about a half-mile to where the campground owners lived. It was only 4:30 am and the lights in their house were not on. I walked and I walked until six am. Then the lights were on, thank God, and they unlocked the cabin door for me.

After visiting and thanking people for letting me stay at the campground, I let anybody that wanted to, ride the bike. After that, I took off and continued my journey.

Again, I had no connections anywhere. I just went down the road on a highway toward Milford. Every little town where I stop, I find people that wanted to know about the bike and what I am doing and why.

Thursday, October 15, 2015

I travel through small towns. There is beautiful scenery wherever I go. I have lots of time to think and philosophize. Actually, I can't tell you all the things I think about. Everywhere I stop, I always ask if they know a Lion. Once-in-a-while, someone can tell me that they know someone.

I am in Seymour, Indiana. I see a man working in the yard. I ask him if they have a motel in town. "Yes, but I don't know if they still rent rooms. You can go there and find out. Otherwise, there are motels along the interstate highway that is about six miles east of here." I thanked him and went on my way.

I had ridden quite far and I didn't feel like going six more miles, so I went to the one just a few blocks down the road. It was a huge place. In its day it must have been a very prominent place. There was a big, three-story house and, in a horseshoe-like shape, a group one-story motel rooms. I drove in there. I am looking for the office. People were outside. I asked a man where the office is. He kind of shrugged his shoulders as if he didn't really know. He pointed to the three-story building. I rode the Elf over there and talked to a guy unloading stuff off a pickup. I asked where the office is. He said his mother runs it, but she is not there. She won't be back until Monday. "Is there a way I can get a room?" I asked. "Well" he said, "we don't really rent rooms out, but if you're not too fussy, I can show you a place." He took me in the three-story building and onto the second floor. He showed me a room that was full of rubble. A TV was on the floor. He said, "I think that works." I said, "I don't need a TV." The bathroom looked pretty much in shambles. I said, "I will bring my air mattress in and sleep on that. That will be okay, as long as the toilet works and the water runs. I don't need hot water, if that doesn't work. Then he took me to next-door apartment. It was very nicely furnished. "I live here part-time," he told me. Then he opened what looked like a heavy curtain on a small stage. There was a huge bed and something was in the bed, like a mannequin or something. It didn't move. He closed the curtain. I said, "What is that? It looks dead." He went back and looked and closed the curtain again and said, "That's my girlfriend. I wish she was dead." I was getting a little bit scared. It was three in the afternoon and she is still sleeping. She must be on drugs. Those people scare me. I will be staying in the room right next door to her, but I have a dozen angels looking after me. It will be okay.

The guy said, "Let me introduce you to some of the people that live here." He took me to the horseshoe-shaped, one story motel. He introduced me to one lady who he said they called 'Grandma'. "She cooks for all of us." He said, "We had chili, would you like some?" "No, thank you, I ate not too long ago." I said. Then he said, "Let me help you carry your stuff upstairs." So, we got out my air mattress and sleeping bag and a few other things. As we were walking toward the house, 'Grandma' hollered, "Where are you taking her?" He said, "Upstairs." "Why don't you give her the room on the end?" "Well, I could do that." The guy told me, "We use that for storage." We went in there. It was a hundred times better than the room in the big building. I tell you what; I was relieved. There even was a bed in it. I didn't have to use my air mattress.

It was a nice day. We sat outside for a while and visited. He told me about his mother and the owner of that complex, who lives in Florida. Then he complained about his girlfriend and that she costs him a lot of money. He told me that he had been in trouble with the police. He didn't go into detail about it. He said that they are now his friends. He told me that he had a house out in the country, but he stays most of the time with his girlfriend. He says his mother gets a lot of money from the guy that owns that place, but she won't let him (the guy I'm talking to" do things right. He says he knows how to fix about anything. I told him, "You know what you need to do? You have to get away from here; far, far away and don't tell anybody where you're going and start your life over again." I gave him 50 dollars. I said, "That is for you to start your new life with." He didn't stay there that night. I have no clue whatever happened to him. I got up really early the next morning and got the heck out of there.

Friday, October 16, 2015

It was about 7 am. I was looking for a restaurant. About a block away was a guy working on the railroad tracks. I asked him if he knew of a place to eat. He pointed to a restaurant not far away.

Oh, boy, that place was packed with men. Of course, they saw me park my ELF and they all wanted to know about it. Of course, I answered all the questions. The men were Masons. I asked them if they knew a Lion. One of the guys knew the president of a club. "I will call him right now." When he got off the phone, he said, "He was going somewhere, but he is turning around and coming to the restaurant." It wasn't long and he arrived. He was an insurance agent and worked part-time. Some of the Masons had left. We all visited. One of the Mason's wives came and had lunch. I had been there three or four hours. The Mason and his wife invited me to stay at their house. The Lions president asked if I could stay through Saturday. "Yes, I can. I don't have to be anywhere anytime." I was staying with the Mason that night and the insurance agent the next night. Finally, we all left. I went with the Mason to his house. After that, he showed me around town. The next day I rode around with the insurance agent. It was all great. For some reason, it didn't work out to go to the Lions meeting. That was okay. They had a festival in the adjacent town and a parade. I was invited to a lady's house in Vilonia, Indiana. She gave me a new, very fancy American flag for my bike. I stayed there two nights. The parade was on Sunday. It is a really tiny town, but not that day.

Wednesday, October 21, 2015

As I am riding along, I see a guy mowing this huge lawn. He drove toward me on his lawn mower. I stopped and we visited for quite some time. He wrote the next day in the comments on my face book page.

This is what Myron wrote: Bless you Hanna. I will never forget our visit this past Wednesday when you stopped by as I was mowing my lawn. (Between Salem and Palmyra, Indiana) The best of luck to you. Myron Compton

It must be because of all the people like Myron that I don't need to be afraid. They are all in my thoughts as I travel along. Please forgive me, I don't remember everyone's name, but I have all of you always in my mind and in my heart. All of you! YOU ARE ALL MY ANGELS!!!!!!!!!!!!!

I went over the Ohio River into Kentucky. I rode on State Highway 135 to Brandenburg. This was a great road to ride on. It was very quiet.

I HAD A LOT OF TIME TO THINK. ONE CAN THINK A LOT IN A SHORT TIME, BUT WRITING IT IS ANOTHER STORY.

 How I landed in Chatfield, MN

I am going to tell you how I landed in Chatfield, Minnesota. World War II ended in September 1945. Everyone came out of the houses and stood on the side of the road in our village, Borstel and in Verden and, I imagine, everywhere else. I was almost three years old. I can only tell you what was told to me as I was growing up.

We had the British in our area. Their tanks went by our house, rumbling through the streets. People where clapping and screaming,

THE WAR IS OVER!!!! THE WAR IS OVER!!!!

Now this is what I learned in history in school:

The war was over. Hitler was gone. No one is really sure what happen to him. I learned that he killed himself. It doesn't really matter, he was gone. The rules stayed the same. America was going to get rid of the Germans. They thought that everybody was a Nazi. That was not the case at all. In our village, there were not many. They belonged to the so-called PARTY so they could go shopping and they got a little better treatment. My father never belonged to the PARTY. He refused to salute the Nazi flag.

My father somehow got the book, "MEIN KAMPF," before Hitler got voted in. My father told everyone, "Don't vote for him. This is what he is going to do," referring to what he had read in that book. Everyone laughed

at him and said, "That is just a novel." Well, now we know that my father was right, that is what happened.

The British and the Americans went house to house to smoke out the Nazis. People would hide their valuable stuff. They locked up the good dishes and silverware. The soldiers just came in and ransacked some of the places. Our neighbor had a special gun. He crawled, in the middle of the night, to the septic tank and threw the gun in there. That was the kind of fear thy put in us.

The soldiers came to our house. They asked my father if he knew anyone that was a Nazi. He didn't know anyone. He didn't know that a guy four houses down from ours was an "SS" man, secret service Nazi. No one knew he was one of them. He lived his life like any other German. He was never found out. Long after I had come to America, that guy was on his death bed, and, for whatever reason I don't know, he called my father to his bedside and told him that he had been a Nazi "SS" man. He said, "You are very lucky that the Americans came. I had ORDERS to have you and your family loaded on a truck and sent to Siberia." That's why I can say:

AMERICA SAVED MY LIFE

On my journey, people often asked if I was doing what I was doing for a purpose. It was hard for me to keep my composure. Many times, I couldn't talk about it. I would just say that I am trying to promote Lions and their Leader Dog for the Blind. When I could talk about it, I would tell them the story. I tell them that, when they go home and see their friends, they can tell them, "There is a crazy woman on a crazy looking bike thanking the American people for saving her life." And then I said, "Promote the Lions or better yet, become a Lion."

POST-BULLETIN, Saturday, December 11, 1999

Letters to the Editor

America saved her life

Thank you to all the World War II vets.

I am overwhelmed with emotion as I am writing this letter of gratitude and thanks to you and the people of the United States.

I was born in 1942 in northern Germany, just an infant when you put your life on the line for me and many others. My life was literally saved by you.

Many years after the war, my father was called to our dying neighbor's bedside. Our neighbor confessed to my father that he had been a Nazi SS man and that he had gotten orders to load us on a truck, but just then the Americans came and the war came to an end.

We were not Jewish, but we belonged to an independent Lutheran church, we said prayers at the table and my father would not salute the Nazi flag.

Not only did you save my life, I had the privilege in 1961 to immigrate to this country and enjoy living among the greatest and kindest people in the world. I will be forever indebted to you.

God bless the United States of America, my home.

Hanna Elshoff
13134 Mill Creek Road
Chatfield

After the Americans decided to help us rebuild Germany, life got much better. Especially after I left in 1961. My father sold land for development. He bought other land back. The cold war was in big swing. We are as close to communist Germany as Minnesota is to Iowa. My father was always afraid that the Russians would take one big step and we would be gone. Since I was already living in the USA, he sent my bachelor brother, Manfred, over to America with a hand full of money. Manfred stayed with us in Rochester. We got a realtor and looked for a farm. He found a 169 acre farm just outside of Chatfield, Minnesota. I don't remember how much he paid for it, but he bought it. It was in 1972, just before the land prices took a huge leap. Manfred had plenty money left. He bought a brand new Oliver tractor, a Chevy pickup, and two Holstein cows that had just calved. He made his life in Chatfield. After a year, my mother and father came to see him and the farm. My parents loved the farm. They said, "That is a whole village." It was the beginning of May in 1973. We had a snowstorm. Manfred and my parents came back to Chatfield from somewhere, I don't know where they had been, but they got stuck on the hill. Manfred got his tractor and got them back to the farm. That didn't discourage them at all. They just loved the farm and Chatfield. Manfred, on the other hand, wanted to go back with them or he said he would die.

My dad asked me to move onto the farm and do with it as I saw fit. Manfred went back to Germany with them and my husband and I moved onto the farm and that's how I came to Chatfield.

My parents are both gone. After a few years, I got divorced. My husband was terribly abused as a child. He told me all about that. He told me not to let him become that way. I learned that no one can keep anyone else from doing anything. One can be supportive, but no one can change a person. Life wasn't very easy for me. Thank goodness the farm was not in my name or I would have had to give it up in the divorce and I would have been on the street. Everything works out the way it's supposed to.

I SURVIVED! Thanks to Betty and Lowell Wooner, my neighbors; Charlie Johnson, the banker; the Implement dealers, Palmer and Audrey Borgen; and many others.

I SURVIVED! A BIG THANKS TO JANELLE WHO IS TEN YEARS OLDER THAN MY DAUGHTER ANDREA!

 Janelle comes into my life

How Janelle came into my life.

We still lived in Rochester. Our son, Karl was four years old and Andrea was almost two. We were licensed foster parents for infants that were up for adoption. The last baby we had was Tommy, who was born with a liver disease. (I wrote about Tommy when I was getting the ELF trailored by Bonnie Shay in Minnesota.) We got Tommy shortly before social service called me about Janelle. She was already 11 years old. I turned them down because, at 11 years old, they are usually already pretty messed up. They called me a second time; they were desperate. They told me that it was an unusual situation. I agreed to take her.

Janelle's story!

Janelle's mother's first husband died at a young age. She had five children. Most of them were out of school. She met Milton Hart, who was in his sixties. He had never been married. Doris was in her forties. They got married and decided to have a child. They had a girl and named her Janelle.

Janelle's mother, Doris, had already suffered from crippling arthritis. A pregnancy on top of a chronic disease can make it much worse, as it did in her case. When Janelle was 10, the doctors came up with an operation to do on Doris's hip to relieve the pain. It was a new procedure. Well, it didn't work out for Doris. She never got out of the wheelchair. Milton was, by that time, 70 years old and couldn't take care of his wife and an 11-year-old daughter. He and Doris both had to go to the nursing home in Stewartville, MN. That's when they called me about caring for Janelle.

One of Janelle's half-brothers, Doug, and his wife would have loved to have taken her, but they could not afford it. At that time, family members

who were willing to take care of a relative got no assistance from social services or the county. Thank goodness that has changed, as far as I understand. We didn't get paid much for caring for Janelle, but, her health and dental care were taken care of and she had a clothing allowance.

She never caused me a minute's trouble. I don't know what I would have done without her. She is now 59. She has been like my right arm. My daughter Andrea is ten years younger.

When Janelle was dating Kevin, her parents were still alive. One time, I asked her if she had any interest in getting married. I told her that, if so, perhaps she should do that when her parents were still alive. She wasn't so sure about him. I said, "You'll get used to him." She still, in a humorous way, holds that against me.

It was a very nice wedding. Janelle danced with her father. Of course, her mother was in a wheelchair.

Janelle and Kevin put a mobile home next to the farmhouse. We are one happy bunch. They took over the milking for many years until we couldn't afford it anymore. We were going two steps forward and three steps back, so we sold the cows.

Two years after Kevin and Janelle were married, they went to see her parents at the Stewartville Care Center in the afternoon. It was the day after Thanksgiving. Janelle called me to inform me that they were going to be a little late for milking because they had put Doris in the hospital and that her dad was lonesome. I said, "Bring him home to us." He was physically in pretty good shape and he loved it on the farm. They packed him up and brought him to the farm. Kevin and Janelle did the milking and, since they always ate at my house, we all ate together that night. Milton thoroughly enjoyed himself that evening.

Check with Janelle to see if can put her wedding picture in here

The next morning Kevin and Janelle went out to milk the cows. Kevin went back in the house to check on Milton. He had died. He just went in his sleep.

Everyone was afraid to tell Doris that Milton had died. The day of his funeral, the minister went to the hospital in the morning and told Doris that Milton had passed away. That night she died.

DOESN'T EVERYTHING WORK OUT THE WAY IT'S SUPPOSED TO?

 Jon Van Loon

Let me introduce you to Jon Van Loon.

I don't know what year it was, but our Veterinary Clinic had hired a new veterinarian, Dale Timm. Dale was a bachelor and when he came to treat a cow, he would talk about his girlfriends. Then, he would bring them to my house to see what I thought of them. He did this with all but the one he married. Anyway, one of Dales rejects, Lucy, asked me if I had a place for her horse; I did. When she brought the horse out to my place, she introduced me to Jon Van Loon. They would help with my wood splitting and a few other things. I had horses at that time. They would go horseback riding. After a time, Jon broke up with Lucy. He asked if he could still come out. He was into taking pictures of native flowers and plants in the 60 acres of woods on the farm.

I had been on my own and milking a few cows and working at night for the trucking company, International Transport, in Rochester for some time. The state milk inspector was due to come and inspect the barn and the milk house. I was in the barn getting prepared for the inspector's visit by washing off the stainless steel milk line. Jon came out of the woods where he had been taking pictures. I was desperate for help. I asked Jon if he could help me clean the lines. Jon is 6 foot 4 inches tall and he could just stand there and wipe the lines off. I, on the other hand, had to stand on a bucket, water running down my arms. Jon was great help. After that, he would call practically every weekend and ask if I had work for him and if he could bring some of his co-workers from the Mayo Clinic with him. The

answer was always, "Yes. Sure. Just remember the service is lousy around here." That was how I met Jon. He helped so much. Of course, the horses were an attraction. I never had time to ride them.

Jon pitched a lot of manure. I had calves in every building. The calves would leave the building, but the manure stayed until Jon and his new girlfriend or co-workers came.

One Saturday, he came and told me that he had met a guy from Agri-news at a bar. Agri-news was a new weekly newspaper for farmers. When Jon told him that he was going the next day to a woman farmer's, the guy asked if I would mind being interviewed for the Agri-news. Jon asked me the next day. I said, "Of course, that would be okay."

Find and insert image of agri-news article of November 1982 and get permission to use it.

Jon came often until he bought his own house. That was about the same time that Kevin and Janelle took over the milking.

Years go by. Sometimes I would not see Jon for a year or two. One time, he commented, "No matter how long I am gone, this place always stays the same." I took that as a huge compliment.

Jon was working in pharmacology. He had been there for a long time. He decided to go to Mayo Medical School. That's where he met his wife, Lori Bates. I was invited to graduation when Jon and Lori completed Med School. I was kind of out of the loop as to what was going on in Jon's private life. I had no idea that he had a girlfriend.

If you ever have an opportunity to go to a Doctor's graduation, go. It is beautiful and elaborate. The speaker, former U.S. Surgeon General Dr. Antonia Novello, was fantastic. In 1990, during the Bush Administration, Dr. Novello became the first woman and first Hispanic to hold the country's top medical position. Dr. Novello beckoned 67 Mayo Foundation graduates to take their "gown to town" and help others. "Service is the rent we pay for living," she said in a wide-ranging commencement speech. "There's far too much 'What can I get?' out there rather than 'What can I give?' Reach out to all types of people, including the homeless, poor mentally ill and other "voiceless" groups."

Shortly after graduation, Jon and Lori got married.

After a few years, they had their first child, Caleb. At that time, I was working during the day taking care of Connie Rehm. Connie was afflicted severely with MS. Connie and her husband, Bill and their teenage daughter, Chris lived on a farm midway between Chatfield and Rochester. I called this second job an assignment. I get jobs in very peculiar ways. I don't look for them. I just want to help were I can. I didn't want any pay for caring for Connie, but Bill insisted on giving me something. He gave me corn for my cows. It was a great assignment. We had a lot of laughs. After two years, Connie went into a nursing facility, so that assignment came to an end.

Jon Van Loon and Lori Bates and their graduation of medical medicine

I was down to my regular job and had time to meet Caleb. He was almost a year old. I called Jon and asked when would be a good time to stop? "Anytime, I took a 3 month leave of absence from work." I went after I got done at Madonna Towers, met the cute little boy, visited for a while, had some coffee and went home. That was great. I didn't get so dreadfully sleepy, as I usually did when I didn't take a nap after working all night. Jon told me that they were in the process of looking for a nanny.

I started stopping at Jon's quite often because it kept me awake. After I stopped about the fourth or fifth time, Jon asked me if I could take care of Caleb. "Sure," I said. "But I don't want to get paid because you have helped so much on the farm and I never paid you." They wouldn't hear of it. "Well," I said, "All these years I usually had two jobs and I have stuck everything I earned from both jobs back into the farm. I tell you what, I have this dream to go to Australia in four years to the Summer Olympics, but you have to manage my money or I will pay bills with it."

That's how I became part of the Bates/Van Loon family. After three years, they had another baby, Greta.

It was a great life. During the day I took care of the very young and at night the very old.

I got to the Olympics and many other places. I had joined the Lions club, which took me to Japan to an International Lions convention and lots of other places.

It was a long assignment. Caleb and Greta are both in college. Greta is in her first year at St. Olaf in Northfield, Minnesota. She insisted on being the editor for this book. I gladly obliged, but that was before we realized that as a college student, she doesn't have the time. Thanks, anyway, Greta!

Back to my journey.

I am heading for Kentucky now.

Kentucky

The roads I traveled in Kentucky

Horses in Verden

I have another emotional moment as I come into Kentucky. I have never been in Kentucky before.

I love horses. Verden, where I grew up in Germany, is known for the Han-noveraner horses. If anybody goes to Germany for horses, they go to the little city of VERDEN AN DER ALLER (on the river Aller). That's where one can get riding lessons and driving lessons. All my dad would let me ride was a workhorse. After we got a tractor, that was all we needed. We used it for pulling the drag and small stuff like that. When I was nine or

ten years old, I am not quite sure, but I was very young, I liked working with the horse.

Around that time, we had two horses. One was totally white. My dad always said it was from the Lipizzaner. When music was playing, it would dance. We had that horse until it died.

We didn't have any land behind the house. We had to take the horses or milk cows through the village of Borstel, which was annexed into Verden after I left.

That's what it looks like when they take the cows down the
road to the pasture.

I wasn't very old at all when my brother would put me on one of the horses and I would ride it home from the pasture in the evening. One time, the neighbor kids purposely scared the horse and I fell off. It wasn't far to go home, but I guess I cried all the way.

My sister was older than I and she always helped my mother. My father couldn't do much, he was always sick. I liked to harness the horse and load up the drag on the wagon, go through the village to the field, unload the drag, unhook the horse from the wagon and hook it onto the drag and drag the field. I worked until almost dark. When I got home, my dad would praise me and praise me. That felt so good that I always wanted to

do that. The neighbors saw me by myself on that wagon and they would wonder about that. They would talk to my dad. In low German. "WERE DAT DEENE LUTHCHE DEERN ON DEN WOGEN?" Was that your little girl on that wagon? It felt so, so good. That is just to show, praising children is all it takes to train them. My dad didn't have the energy to do the work. My brother Hans went off to Bremen to work and Manfred was doing other things. My sister was working in Verden in a household.

 Celiac Sprue

IF WE ONLY WOULD HAVE KNOWN ABOUT CEALEAC SPRUE!!!!!!!!

Celiac wasn't understood in this country 30 years ago. My sister had it. As an adult, she has lived in several different countries and was always treated for chronic colitis. They gave her a lot of Cortizone shots, among other things, which are bad for a person. It wasn't until she moved to Canada that a nurse or a doctor or someone said to her, "Try not to eat any bread for a week and see how you feel." In one week, she knew that she could not eat bread and that the bread had something to do with her getting sick. That was about 40 years ago. She is still alive and lives in Canada. She is 84, but she suffers a lot. She gets diarrhea from a lot of things. She doesn't complain.

My daughter, Andrea, lived in Cleveland, Ohio for a few years. She was 22 years old. I was working at Madonna Towers from 10 pm to 6:15 am. One evening, about 9 pm, I was just about to go to work, when the phone rang. It was Andrea. She said that there was something terrible wrong with her. At that time, she didn't have any Insurance. She had just had her blood tested to see if she had cancer or something like that. They didn't find anything wrong with her. I asked her all kinds of questions. I was a little bit in a hurry; I usually leave at 9 pm. Finally, she said something about having diarrhea. Off the top of my head, I just said, "Don't eat any bread for about a week and see if that makes a difference." After a week, she called me and was excited. The bread had been making her sick.

At that time, Mayo Clinic had just come out with the Mayo Clinic FAMI-LY HEALTH BOOK. We had a copy of that book on our station at work. As soon as I got to work, I got that book out and started looking for gluten intolerance. It is an autoimmune disease. It is called Celiac Sprue.

IT IS HEREDITARY!!!!!

Sometimes babies are born with it, but most of the time it shows up in young adults.

Later on, Andrea moved back to Chatfield and she lives a pretty normal life. She just has to stay gluten-free.

We assumed that my dad had CELIAC SPRUE

The Burgermeister (Mayor), did all he could to hold my father back from going into the Nazi army, because he knew how sick he was, but my father had to go anyway. He was only in the army two days. After they had given him all the necessary shots, his whole body swelled up and they had to cut his uniform off. They put him in the army hospital. They said, "We'll make a soldier out you yet." They knew that he was against Hitler. He was in the hospital a year and a half or so. They thought he was going to die. They carried him home on a blanket. He couldn't walk. He had gotten very thin. A neighbor said that the only person that was that thin was a dead person.

My mother gave him blueberry juice to drink when he got home; and the second day mashed potatoes with lots of butter, a soft-boiled egg and blueberries and the juice. After about a week, he could get out of the bed. Of course, he was very weak. He wanted to go outside and look at the fields. I remember pushing him on the bicycle; he didn't have enough strength to pedal.

My father was a very optimistic person and had a very strong belief in God. He felt good when I would push him on the bike and he would whistle. He always whistled some happy sounding hymn.

He went through those spells several times a year. One time, I remember, they took him to Verden to the hospital. I don't remember how old I was; 8, 9, or 10. When they wheeled him through the FLUR (the foyer), he said to us, "Goodbye. I won't see you anymore." He thought he was dying of

cancer. My sister cried. On the other hand, I'm ashamed to admit it, but I was kind of happy inside because he was always sick. (This is the only time I have ever confessed that.) He slowly got his strength back.

Blueberries grew in the woods in our area. My mother had people pick many blueberries for her. She canned about 50 jars every year. They were only for my dad.

Over the years, he would never eat that heavy Schwarzbrot (German bread). He would only eat bread like French bread. We had no idea that it was the gluten in the grain.

Only when we had company would we have coffee bean coffee; it was very expensive. He wouldn't drink the coffee bean coffee; he would always drink the coffee made from grain. You can still buy that in Germany. The Germans eat a lot of bread. As kids, we would drink the roasted grain coffee. It tastes pretty good.

In spite of all the times he was so sick, my father lived to be 70 years old.

When Andrea came back to Minnesota about 25 years ago, there was very little gluten free food to find, but now, almost every store has a special corner where you can find it.

Just for your information: Gluten can cause all kinds of problems. One can have gluten intolerance. It is hard to detect, but worth your while to test it out. I personally know a good friend that had severe depression and found out that she was gluten intolerant. She has been okay ever since.

There is good gluten free magazine called "LIVING WITHOUT." Ten years ago, I read in that magazine that 97% of the people that have Celiac don't know it.

My daughter has Celiac, and she does ok.

Enough Day dreaming for now.

Thursday, October 22, 2015

I crossed the Ohio River. I am in Brandenburg, Kentucky. I got a nice room at Abe's Cabins. I got a call from friends that I met on my journey in Minnesota. They are on vacation. They are on their way home and they can stop by and see me. I will wait for them and stay another day.

Friday, October 23, 2015

It was about noon or so when Bonnie, her husband, and some of her relatives from Minnesota came to see me. It was great to have people that I had met earlier on my journey come for a visit. I really enjoyed the couple of hours we spent together.

I rode around in Brandenburg. It is a very pretty town. I went to sleep quite early that evening. At about midnight, there was quite the cackle right next door to me. A couple of ladies where having a good time. Once they went to sleep, it was nice and quiet.

I got up very early, about 5 am, today. I started loading up my bike. The one lady from next door was sitting outside knitting or something like that. I started talking to her. She didn't want to wake up her friend. Then she told me that they were going to her brother's farm. They were having some kind of children's day and demonstration of some sort there. She had two rabbits in the car. She told me that I could go; that anybody could go. She gave me directions. We visited some more. She asked me about the bike and so on. We left at about the same time. They were to go out to eat first. Her brother's farm is near Gaston, KY. I got there about 11 am. There was hardly anybody there. It was raining. The farm was set up for kids to play; very creative. I was impressed. It started raining harder. We went and sat in a shed and visited. Later, it led up some. The two ladies came and set up their goods. The whole afternoon, the weather was not nice. They told me that if I could stay overnight, the weather be would better tomorrow and I would see a crowd. I stayed overnight on the farm. That was great. Sunday was quite different. It was busy. I had a very good time. First thing in the morning, we had to deliver a big sheet cake to some teaching nuns from Malta. They had been in Malta fifty years teaching at the catholic school. After they were retired, they were sent back to the USA. The church had a celebration for them. In the late afternoon, they came to Robert's family farm, where the Kid's Day was being held. It was a lot of fun to visit with them and their cute little dog.

Monday October 26, 2015

My destination was the Rough River Dam State Park.

A piece of cake; less than 40 miles from here. Well, a lot of time to day-dream. The weather was dreary. And the scenery was not all that great. They've had some fires in the past. I rode and I rode and I asked questions. Hardly any towns on my route. Then, I saw a sign for Rough River Dam State Park. There was one house by the turn. I stopped there and asked if that was the right turn and how far it was to the park. My battery was getting low. The resident said, "About 8 miles." If there are a lot of hills between here and the park, I think I am going to run into trouble. He gave me his phone number and said, "If you run into trouble, give me a call." I thanked him and went on my way. I made it. I was glad.

Let me tell you, the Kentucky State Parks are well run by the state. They are beautiful. The cabins are like nice motel rooms. The restaurant tables had tablecloths on them. It was very nice.

It was raining very hard when I arrived. Everybody was looking and watching me ride in. Like I told you earlier, I barely get wet riding the ELF. I signed in and found a plug-in for my bike. Everything is under cover. That place had a lot of meeting rooms. There were several different groups of people there for various meetings.

The next morning, when I looked at my bike, I had a flat tire. I pumped it up and, right away, it went flat again. I called BETTER WORLD. After about an hour, a truck came and picked the ELF and me up and took us to the bicycle doctor in Leitchfield. The bike shop was called Embry's Bikes and Boards. The owners' names were Joyce and Rick. The people at the park must have called ahead and told them that they were bringing an unusual contraption. When we got there, the newspaper person was there waiting for us.

It was a small town. The guy at the bicycle shop had called District Governor Lion Paul Witten already. He came in to visit with me. They had a gossip table with coffee cups. It was great for visiting.

I guess the damage was quite severe. I needed new tires. They ordered them from Organic Transit. I said, "Can't you fix it so that I can ride it?" "Yes, we can do that." "Do you have a motel in town?" "We do, but we have a beautiful fairground and just built a state-of-the-art shower room. If you don't mind, you can sleep in it. I am on the board, I can give you permission. You wait an hour and I'll show it to you." That was great. He fixed the flat tire so I could ride around.

I went to the gas station and got some food for in the morning. I rode around on the fairgrounds. There were people jogging and walking. A gentleman came in a car with his two dogs. He took the dogs out of the car to go for a walk. Of course, he wanted to know about my bike. I told him all he wanted to know. I, also, told him that I was waiting for Rick from the bike shop to come and open the shower building for me. I plan on sleeping in there. The guy left with his two dogs. It wasn't long and he came back. He said he talked to his wife and that I could come home with him. He would call Rick at the bike shop and tell him that he doesn't need to come.

What a blessing. Everyone has been just so nice to me. But this couple, I don't know, Cathy was a character. She had so many stories to tell. I told her she had to write a book. Oh boy, the stories are a lot more interesting then what I have to tell. Plus, she has a lot of education. She is very smart.

I stayed with Cathy and Larry for four days. I don't know what all I can tell you. All I can say is that everyone in that town was great. Just like everywhere else.

Goodbye and goodbye, again. It doesn't get any easier as the time goes on.

Monday, November 2, 2015

I am on my way to Bowling Green, KY.

I finally made it to Lion Lyndell Graves. It was a lot farther then I thought and very stressful riding. Bowling Green is a much bigger city then I imagined. I made it to his house, which was right on the highway that I was on. He escorted me to the Super 8 Motel. It was only 2:30 pm, but I was glad I didn't have to go any farther.

Lyndell Graves who escorted me to the motel, which
had reservations for me.

After getting checked in, I asked if they had an electrical outlet some-where. They didn't know of any. I asked them if it was alright for me to see if I could find one. I found one behind the building. There was no one around. I plugged in my bike. I went inside and reported that I had found one and then I went to my room and rested until Lyndell picked me up and took me to a Lions Zone Meeting.

I always said, the only reason people talked to me was because of the ELF. This time, no one saw me with the ELF. Neither did anyone see the ELF behind the building. Nobody talked to me. The same was true in the morning at breakfast. No one even said, "Good morning." After breakfast, I went and brought the bike to the front of the motel. Then, they came out of the woodwork. I let people ride it around in the parking lot. It was a lot of fun, but I was right; the journey is what it is because of the ELF. AND THAT'S OK!

Some of the people at the motel were going to go to the Corvette Museum in Bowling Green. In February of 2014, a massive sinkhole formed in the Museum and 8 Corvettes fell in. Tourists can see those Corvettes, as well as an outline on the floor showing where the sinkhole had been. When the people at the motel spied the ELF, they delayed leaving for the Museum in order to talk to me and take turns riding the bike.

Tuesday, November 3, 2015

I was close to Franklin, Kentucky. I had to get off the highway to find out where the closest motel might be. I stopped at a gas station. A young couple with two young children came in looking for the person that might belong to the ELF. They figured that I belonged to the Lions with a Lions flag on the bike. When they saw me with the Lions emblem on my shirt, they knew that I belonged to the bike. Thy talked to me and told me that they were Lions. It was so exciting. We visited for a little bit. I gave them my e-mail address and they left.

I found a cute little motel run by people from India. I always like those motels. They are usually very clean and not very expensive.

Wednesday, November 4, 2015

I looked at my phone and I had a message from that wonderful couple I met last night at the gas station. They invited me to Mc Donald's for breakfast. I was so excited to be able to visit with them and to exchange stories and thoughts. It is so encouraging to find young people who are Lions.

So, to my Lion friends, there it is: HOPE. Never, never give up. We need to keep the Lions' spirit alive.

Albert Schweitzer says:

I don't know what your destiny will be, but one thing I know: The only ones among you who will be really happy, are those who have sought and found a way to serve.

Very fitting for Lions.

This delightful couple followed me to the restaurant.
The father happened to be a Lion.

Now on to Tennessee…..

The roads I traveled in Tennessee

I don't recall a lot of what happened as I rode through Tennessee, except going through Nashville. I didn't put anything on my Facebook page.

This is what I remember:

I am trying to go through Nashville, Tennessee. I drive around and around before I finally stopped. A couple of motorcycle drivers saw me standing around trying to figure out which way to go. They said they would drive ahead of me and show me which way to go. I followed them. We went right through the middle of Nashville. It was a good day, because it was the day Joe Biden was visiting Nashville. There were police everywhere. Everybody was watching their Ps and Qs. I got through Nashville just fine. The two motorcycle riders waved goodbye once they knew that they had me on the right track.

I was going to Franklin, Tennessee. I stayed with Michelle Mills. They are great people. Everywhere I go I feel at home.

Franklin is a nice town. I was going to visit the Lions club there and, hopefully, see Karen Taylor Good, but, for some reason it didn't happen. The reason I really wanted to visit the club, was because one of the members, Karen Taylor Good, was a member of the Franklin Lions club. I had heard her speak in Milwaukee at the US-Canada Forum. She is a singer, song writer and speaker. I have gone to several Lions functions. In my opinion, she was the best speaker I have ever heard. I remember one of the speeches she wrote a song about. A fisherman, whenever he caught a big fish, threw it back in the water. She finally asked him, "Why do you throw the big fish back in the water?" He got his frying pan out. It was too small for the big fish. She said, "Get a bigger pan." She compared that with one's dreams. Don't worry about your dreams being too big. Don't throw them out; get a bigger pan.

Another thing that Karen said; When they asked her if she would like to become a Lion, she said that she didn't belong to anything. She said she was not a joiner, but she joined the Lions in Franklin.

I highly recommend her music, but you have to listen to her words. You won't regret it. If I knew that she was going to speak somewhere, I would go there. Her name is KAREN TAYLOR GOOD.

I spent several days in Franklin with Michelle and her great family. I rode around on my ELF. I Never went to the Franklin Lions meeting. I never saw Karen. It wasn't meant to be.

I rode my bike through Tennessee. I had lots of time to daydream.

 ### My Health

As I begin about my health, I want to note we have very good doctors. I am not at all trying to make them look bad or anything like that. But my body is just not normal. It reacts opposite to the way perhaps most bodies react.

55 years ago, when I went for my first checkup to the Mayo Clinic with my first pregnancy, Dr. Kempers left the room for a very long time. When he came back, he said, "What I am fussing about is your blood type. You have A positive but your body reacts negative. If you ever need a blood transfusion, don't let them give you positive blood."

Over the years, I forgot about it. I have periodically asked doctors about it. No one knew about anything like that. When I wrote about my health, I didn't think about my blood type, that is until a week ago. I thought I would mention it. If someone knows anything about that, please let me know.

My Facebook page: Hanna's Dream Ride
I would greatly appreciate a comment.

As I am riding along, I think about my health. I have a rather unusual body. It does not like medicine. It reacts, mostly, the opposite of what the medicine is supposed to make it do. If the medicine is to make you sleepy, it keeps me awake, and so on.

People along the way ask me how old I am. I gladly tell them, because I still can. I am not dead yet. I don't have a problem with looking older. That doesn't bother me. However, one does get closer to death as we get older. No one gets out of here alive.

In 1985, my daughter Andrea spent a year in Borstel, Germany with my mother and bachelor brother. Karl was in college in Rochester. Janelle and Kevin were milking cows and I was working, at that time, at International Transport Trucking Company answering the phone. It was a pretty big company. I don't know exactly how many employees they had., I guess about one hundred plus lots of drivers and contractors.

They went from key punch to direct data entry. I worked from 4 pm until 11 pm. After 6 pm, there were just two of us left. The drivers had to call every day with a "progress" report. They would tell us their unit number, what they were hauling, where they were going and when they had to deliver the freight. I am telling you, they speak a different language and in a different manner. At first, that had me almost in tears. After I learned how to talk to them, they couldn't get ahead of me. When we entered their unit number, the first thing we saw on the screen was their messages, so we could let them know who had called for them. The two of us were kind of trouble shooters. You never knew what, or who, was wanted when the phone rang. One thing good about that job, I was salaried, as opposed to hourly, and I had very good insurance for the first time since I was divorced.

Opal worked with me at International Transport in Rochester. She had to have surgery; they found cancer on her ovary. When she came back to work, she kept saying she didn't feel good. She couldn't keep any food down. I asked her how she knew that she had cancer. She told me that she just happened to go for a checkup, and that's how they found it. She died a month later.

I hadn't had a checkup since the kids had been born. . I thought I better have a checkup. I went for a checkup. Wouldn't you know, the doctor found a cyst on my ovary. I had to have that removed. It was more complicated than they thought to begin with. They had to remove all my female parts. It was the best thing that ever happened to me. I suffered a lot from PMS. In those days, they kept a patient at least one week after surgery. When I left the hospital, I was told that I had to take hormone replacement the rest of my life. I was home a month and began to have terrible back aches. I never in my life had a problem with my back. I went to the clinic and asked if it could possibly be from those pills. I was assured that there was no way that it could be from the hormone replacement pills and that I must take them, because it prevented all kinds of stuff including cancer. They gave me some pain pills. I took one of them. It made me feel so awful that I never took another one. I flushed the rest of them down the toilet. I also quit taking the hormone replacement pills; I don't remember what the name of them was. My back pain finally went away. After a year, I went back to the doctor as I had been told. I got the same sermon. They gave me a different kind of hormone replacement pills and a different dose. The same thing happened, except, this time, the pain was in my ankles. Again, I went back to the doctor. They promised me that it could not come from the medicine. They always had a name for what was wrong and a way they could fix it. The next year, I went back, again, as I had been told. I quit taking the pills, which made the pain go away, but this time it took longer. The fourth year I switched from doctoring at the Mayo Clinic to the Olmsted Medical Center, thinking that they would listen to me. I got the same sermon from them. Again, they gave me different pills. This time, I got bunions. I could not wear shoes, unless they were very soft. It was very bad. They told me they could operate on them. Again, I stopped taking the pills. This time it took almost a half a year be-

fore it didn't hurt anymore. I still have a little bunion left foot. The fifth year, again, they gave me different pills, and a different dose. This time, first one thumb would hurt and later jump out of the socket. Then the other thumb would start. I always showed it to Janelle, because I would question my own sanity. I quit taking the pills and I promised myself I would not go to a doctor unless I broke a leg. In 1988, when I started to work at Madonna Towers, I had both thumbs wrapped in ace wraps. I couldn't even open the car door, unless I had ace wraps around the thumbs. It took a whole year before they didn't hurt any more.

My boss at Madonna Towers told me I HAD to get a flu shot. I told them to look at my record and see how often I had called in sick. I told them that, if they make me take the flu shot and I get sick, it will be on their dime. So, I never got a flu shot, and I never got sick. One of my coworkers got a shot for the first time and she was sick all winter. She had never been sick before.

All was good until October 10, 2008. I was 65 years old. I had a stroke in the middle of a speech I was giving at a Toastmasters speech contest. I wrote about my stroke at the beginning of my book when I rode past the cemetery.

The stroke was caused by a brain bleed (My own analysis as to why I had the stroke). The doctors had checked me from head to toe. I have a good heart. I didn't have any blockage anywhere. My cholesterol was impressive. My blood pressure was way too high. I knew that. I controlled that by eating 3 sticks of celery a day. But, after a while, I kept losing track of the celery. Anyway, a couple of years went by.

The day of the speech contest arrived. First of all, I drank way too much coffee. Not to keep me awake, but, when I eat something, which is usually bread with peanut butter and bananas, I drink coffee. Secondly, like always, I was sleep deprived. On that day, a Friday, after working all night, I took Greta to school. After that I slept a couple hours. For two years, I had intended to visit a lady that had once lived at Madonna Towers. I had done her a favor the first night she stayed at Madonna Towers and she never forgot it. One day, after she moved out, she stopped by Madonna Towers to see some friends. Of course, I wasn't there. She left a note

with the day shift asking me to come and see her. After two years, the day of the speech was the day I decided to visit her. She offered me coffee and banana bread, which I enjoyed. Then, it was time to pick up Greta. I had made arrangements with Lori so that I could leave work at her house a little earlier than normal because the drive to Frontenac to the speech contest would take about an hour. When I got to Frontenac, I was early. A few other people were there. We went to a bar/restaurant and I had, you guessed it, more coffee and a baked potato with sour cream and whatever else. At the speech contest, they had snacks and cake and more coffee.

Now I have to tell you something about my Pancreas, which I had learned about ten years prior to this day from a new-found friend, who had childhood diabetes.

Since my pregnancy with Andrea, I get dizzy when I am hungry, or after I eat breakfast in the morning. Occasionally, I would mentioned it to the doctor, "Why do I get dizzy after I eat breakfast?" I never got an answer. I guess he didn't know. When my friend, Jean was at our house, we were having lunch, and just in conversation, we were talking about her diabetes. I asked her how she felt when she gave herself too much insulin. "Oh, I get sweaty and weak and dizzy." I said, "That's funny. That is how I feel sometimes after I eat breakfast and sometimes in the middle of the day." Jean said, "You are the opposite of me. My pancreas does not work at all and yours works too much. You have to live like a diabetic; eat often and try to stay away from sweets. When you are somewhere where you can have your blood sugar tested, and you feel like that, have them check it. Also, drink orange juice."

I followed her advice. One night at work, I was so dizzy I had to sit down. I had the nurse check my blood sugar. It was down to 50. There was my answer.

Now back to my stroke. Everything I ate the day of the speech was bad for me. Plus, I had the nervousness of having to give a speech. All of that was too much for my blood vessel. That is what I think. That's why I had my stroke.

Now I am in the doctors' hands. They saved my life. If I hadn't been where I was, well, maybe I wouldn't have had the stroke. We will never know. All that happens is for a reason.

I was told that the whole group at the speech contest, about 40 people, were upset. I was calm as a cucumber, because I was out of it. The only thing that I remember is thinking 'I am going to die'. I wasn't afraid at all. I told myself, "Just relax. I am not going to make to 2052. It's okay. Just relax." That's all I remember thinking. The ambulance took me to Red Wing Hospital, which is associated with the Mayo Clinic in Rochester. Evidently, they stopped the bleeding. They were going to air lift me to Rochester. I remember hearing someone say, "She is stable. She can go by ambulance." I don't remember anything else. I don't remember getting to Rochester or anything. I don't remember my family coming. I don't know how long I was not aware of anything; I think about a day. The nurse would ask me questions like if I knew those people. I couldn't get it together before I fell asleep again. I had to go to the bathroom really bad. They catheterized me and then I was quiet.

I think it was Sunday afternoon when I started to recognized people a little bit, but I could not talk clearly. I thought to myself, 'I guess I have to go to a nursing home.' I could not walk. I could barely talk and I could not feed myself. I wanted to go to Madonna Towers because they had all private rooms. Monday, they put me in rehab. They wheeled me into the workout unit in a wheelchair. It was quite a workout. I went to rehab two times a day for one hour each time. Two days later, I walked with a walker. Ten days later, I walked out of the hospital. I had people around me on the farm; otherwise I could not be by myself.

In November, I had my 66th birthday. I was alive and that was good. I had a long way to go be able to drive and go back to work. My right side was damaged. When I wanted to wipe off the table, the right hand would not go where I wanted it to. After a while, that got better. It was a slow progress.

At first, I went to the doctor every week. I developed a urinary tract infection. I was on diuretic pills, blood pressure pills, Penicillin for the infection and one other pill. Once I was done with the Penicillin, I felt horri-

ble. The infection was not gone. They gave me more Penicillin. That took care of the infection, but I still felt horrible. They finally figured out that I didn't need the diuretic. I never retained fluid.

I took my blood pressure every morning and evening. When I woke up, I took it and it would be close to 200 over almost 100. As soon as I moved around and ate something, it would drop to 145/85. It was that way all the time.

One morning, when I woke up, my pulse was going so fast, I couldn't count it. I went to the doctor. They made an appointment for me at the clinic to have an Electrocardiogram (ECG). Then, they added a beta blocker to my medicine. I took everything just like I was told to.

Two months later, I wanted someone to tell me that I was okay to drive. I paid a company from Minneapolis to send someone to Rochester to give me a driver's test. Even if I failed, I could keep driving with my current license. That was good, because I would be hauling Greta, and sometimes Caleb, around. The lady came from Minneapolis with a car that had controls on both sides. She tested me for three hours. Besides the driving test, she tested my cognitive thinking. Well, I passed it. That evening, I drove to Jon and Lori's to tell them I could come back to work. We were all happy. The family was back together. I, also, went back to work at Madonna Towers.

I never felt right. Working at night in the assisted living unit, most of the work is physical. When I washed the floor, my blood pressure would go so low that I had to sit-down and wait for it to go back up so I could finish my work. The medicine was not working for me.

One day, I saw Dr. Mike Mesick and his wife from Chatfield in a coffee shop. Mike had worked for the Olmsted Medical Center Clinic in Chatfield. He had taken a year off to learn about alternative medicine. Mike, also, belonged to the Chatfield Lions Club. I got to know him through the Lions Club. He asked me how I felt. I told him, "In short, I can't live and I can't die." I asked him if I could come and see him. He said, "Mayo Clinic has alternative medicine. Have your doctor refer you to that department."

I got an appointment with Dr. Tilbert in alternative medicine. We talked for quite a while. I had taken along a four-page chart that my son-in-law had set up for me on narrow-lined paper. The chart included; when I took my medicine, when I took my blood pressure, when I and what I ate, when I slept, and how I felt. I pulled that out of my pocket and said, "I don't know if you are interested in this." He looked at it and said, "That is a researcher's dream. Can I study it for 10 minutes?" "You can keep it." "No," he said, "I'm just going to study it."

When he got done studying it, he came and sat down and said, "We are like a three-legged stool. If one thing is out of balance, the stool falls over. Let's try it without medicine, BUT, I want you to sleep at least six hours." "In one stretch?" I asked. "No, just a total of six hours."He could see from my chart that it would not work for me to sleep 6 hours in one stretch. He asked if I had to work the two jobs. I did have to keep the Madonna Towers job, so I would have health insurance and I was keeping the other job because I love the family.

I, also, had been going to Marylu Miller, a homeopathy therapist. Maybe, now that I am not taking any medicine, her remedies will work better. They did. My blood pressure became more stable.

About the same time, I got a letter from the insurance company. I had been on Medicare since my 65th birthday. I was still working and had insurance through Madonna Towers. I had filled something out wrong. I don't know what, but the insurance company wouldn't pay any more claims for me. The clinic let me know that, and that I could not receive any service from them anymore. I switched to Olmsted Medical Group for my health care. I corrected my mistake with the insurance company, which took a whole day.

I felt much better now that I wasn't taking any medicine. I am no different than anybody else. If it would have worked, I would have still been taking the medicine.

Obviously, conventional medicine does not work for me. If you remember, the hormone replacement didn't work for me. I am glad my body rejected them. Now, they have found out that all of the things the hormone re-

placements were supposed to prevent, they promote. The doctors seldom prescribe them anymore.

Even supplements don't agree with me. Every time I try taking something, my body reacts in a negative way.

MY ADVICE IS: LISTEN TO YOUR BODY!!!!!!!!!!!!

 More About My Health

Another health issue happened in 2014, a year before I went on my Journey. It started with light pain, as usually signals a urinary tract infection. I drank pure cranberry juice, which usually takes care of it. It did, but not totally. It came back in a different kind of burn. I always shared everything going on with me with my coworkers. In the morning, two ladies came in to relieve me and, in the evening, I would relieve the two ladies who had relieved the morning shift. Most of the ladies are older than middle-aged. Of course, I am the oldest.

I would try different things. At first, they would help a little. But then, the pain would return and be a little different than before. It was hard to explain. I went to see Dr. Vicki Dietz in Chatfield to see if she could find anything, like cancer, was causing the pain. She could not see anything unusual. She didn't know what to do about the pain either. I kept going to Marilu. She kept asking me, "What does it feel like? Is it burning, scratching, or (she mentioned other sensations)?" I would say, "All of the above." She would try different remedies. It would help a little at first, and then, it would almost get worse. After a while, I figured out that, after 6 or 7 hours of not eating, the pain would be totally gone. And I mean totally, completely gone. It didn't make any sense at all because that's not where food goes when you eat it.

One day, Lori, our neighbor lady, came over with a Reader's Digest Magazine containing an article that described exactly what I was experiencing. The article was called: The Pain Down There. The lady in the article had

been to 13 doctors. The last one she saw could help her, but he did not cure it. She did get a lot of relief with massage and some other type of therapy. They named the illness: Pelvic Floor Dysfunction.

I would get sooo hungry, I would eat anything. I was in Kasson, MN at a Lions function one evening, and, after eating, the pain was so excruciating, I went out to the parking lot and just ran around in circles. As I was running, it came to me what to tell Marylu about how my pain felt; When I was doing a lot of the farming, we had electric fencing around the woods. The fence would short out because of all the gooseberry bushes. I would mow around the bushes along the fence with a hand mower with a sickle bar in front. When I got done, I would have thousands of scratches all over my arms. I would take a bottle of alcohol and pour it over my arms. At first, it hurts like the devil, but, in a few seconds, it would be gone. The pain I was feeling now for 6 or 7 hours after I ate, was the same as the pain the alcohol had created on my scratches.

When I told Marylu that, she knew what remedy to give me. Two doses, and it was totally gone. I mean totally gone. That was about 4 years ago. I have had no recurrence thus far. What a relief. It took about nine months to figure out exactly what it felt like and how to stop it. I am so relieved.

I am going on to Alabama now.

Alabama

.Elgin
.Town Creek
.Moulton
.Speake
.Cullman
.Hanceville
.Oneonta
.Wattsville
.Pell City Anniston
Childersburg.
.Sylacauga
.Alexander City
Dadeville. Opelika
.Auburn
Salem

The roads I traveled in Alabama

I rode on Highway 101 all the way into Alabama. I stayed in motels along the way. The scenery was mostly repetitious. I came to what looked like an eating place. It had a sign on it that said "WELCOME: BIKERS HEAVEN." You probably know that they meant motorcycles. Well, I thought they meant me. Next to that building was what looked like a motel. I hadn't seen anything else for miles before that and there wasn't going to be anything else for 7 miles. I drove in and stopped and talked to the guy sitting outside. He didn't look, to my opinion, the best. He looked like a 'biker'. Well, he was. He owned that store. I asked what the place next to him was. "That's a restaurant." I visited with him for a while. I told him my name and asked for his. "They call me 'Dog'" he told me. I asked if there was a motel down the road. He said there was nothing except a few campgrounds. He said he could take me there.

The state-owned campground was closed for the year. Then, we went to a commercial campground. They wanted $90 for one night in a cabin. I never spent that much for a hotel room, so I am certainly not going to pay that much for a campsite. "Well," Dog said, "we will go over the bridge. On the other side, there is another campground and I know the owner." The guy at that campground said, "If you have a tent, you can stay here for free." Dog from Biker's Heaven took me back to his place. He didn't tell me that he had called the newspaper and they were wait- ing for me. It was 4 pm by the time we got back. Then, I had the inter- view. It was getting too late for me to go back to the "free" campground. I said, "How about putting the tent up here?" There was a lot of space around there. As he was looking for a level spot for me to put my tent on, I was looking in a bus that was sitting there. I asked him, "What about the bus?" "Oh, that is full of junk." I said, "Come here." I showed him a little area in the bus that was clear. My air mattress would fit there perfectly. That's where I slept that night.

The next morning, I went next door to Bonnie's Country Cafe. They opened at 5 am. The lady said, "What are you doing up so early?" I said, "Just a minute. I have to use the bathroom quick." After that, I told her my whole story. She said, "You could have stayed at my house. I live on the other side of the highway." Dog and I had gone over to the res- taurant the night before, but she wasn't there. I think Dog thought she might invite me to stay at her house.

Later in the morning, Dog came and said to me, "Tell me when you leave. I have something to give to you." I went over to Biker's Heaven and Dog gave me a wonderful, expensive Jacket.

It is just unbelievable the way my journey is taking me.

THANK YOU SO MUCH FOR THAT BEAUTIFUL JACKET!!!!!! I will treasure it forever.

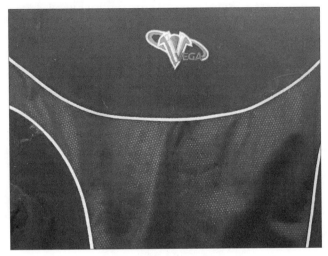

The back of the jacket

John Lennon said, "Life is what happens when you are making other plans!"

Helen Keller said, "The most beautiful and the best things in the world cannot be seen or even touched; they must be felt with the heart."

I am back on Highway 101. I have no idea what and who I am going to meet. I stopped in a place called Town Creek. People at a hardware store saw me coming and were standing outside of the store waiting for me. I stopped and we visited. I asked them if they knew a Lion. Well, I was lucky. One person, Bill King, not only knew a Lion, he knew the President of the Lion Club. Bill called him and he came to where we were visiting. They connected me with Lions in Moulton, Alabama.

Not only did they connected me with Lions in Moulton, but they had a very significant Lion waiting for me when I got there: Lions International Director Jerome Thompson. He was on his way somewhere, but he waited for me. I felt so honored. I call myself a POL, meaning a PLAIN OLD LION. Also, other Lions were there. They looked after me.

I stayed three nights in their beautiful Lions building. During the day, I rode around and met townspeople. It was great.

After that, I am sorry to say, I am not sure where I went. I even lost track of the date.

In the middle of nowhere again, I stopped at a gas station. The same thing happened. Everyone wants to talk to me. I had my phone in my pocket. I must have touched something. I, suddenly, heard a voice. It was Jon Van Loon, my friend in Rochester. He was on facetime. I have no idea how that happened. They didn't call me. It was nice; I got to see the whole family. They were eating dinner. I even got to see Charley, the cat.

 ### The Cat That Was On Death Row

They got the cat from the farm. It was a stray cat and it was on death row. I was catching raccoons in livetraps. One of the traps had a cat in it. My neighbor, Mike, took care of the raccoons. I called him. I said, "There is cat in a trap. Shoot the cat." He said, "I already let the cat out. It is really wild. It ran right into the field." The next day, it came to the house. The other cats chased it away. I put some food close to the house. Well, it wanted to be a housecat. At that time, I already had about 15 cats. Greta's cat had just died. I kept the cat a couple of weeks. Then Greta's dad, Jon, came to the farm, and we got the cat ready for him to take home to Greta.

Sunday, November 15, 2015

I stopped at a gas station 10 miles north of Cullman to get a bite to eat and to ask if there was a motel close by. Just then, I got a call from a Cullman Lion, Jerry Bonner. They had plans for me to stay at Quality Inn. That was wonderful news. It was 3 pm. I got there about 4 pm. Jerry and his wife got there at the same time. It is a wonderful feeling when someone is there to greet you. A little later, we went to eat.

Thank you, thank you, Cullman Lions!

Monday, November 16, 2015

I stayed overnight in a motel in Oneonta and then traveled to Ashville. Allen Shaddock escorted me from Ashville to Pell City. I stayed overnight in Pell City at Allen and his wife, Stacy's, house. In the morning I left their house and got about three or four miles, and one of my tires went flat. I called Allen, and he arranged a truck to haul my bike to Childersburg. I got my bike tire fixed at a car repair place in Childersburg.

I was escorted to Sylacauga, Alabama by Pedro Pino. Pedro is a retired policeman and a devoted Lion. He took very, very good care of me. He didn't just escort me; he helped me find a motel. The motel was under construction, and we talked to some of the construction workers. Pedro invited them to come to a Lions meeting sometime.

The year the Lions held their first International Convention, they invited Ann Sullivan to speak, but not Helen Keller. Ann Sullivan took it upon herself to bring Helen Keller along and let her do the talking. Helen asked the Lions to be the "Knights of the Blind." Since then, the International Lions Clubs have taken that on as their main project.

Helen Keller's birthplace is in Alabama. Lion Pedro told me about an artist that was creating a sculpture of Helen Keller and her very talented teacher, Ann Sullivan

Besides helping me so much in Tuscumbia, Lion Pedro connected me with Lion Angela Hollis in Midland, Georgia. That was a big thing for me, as you will learn when I get to Georgia.

I am on my way out of Alabama and on to Georgia now. I have been riding on a four-lane road with wide shoulders, which are great for me, as long as the rumble strips aren't too close. I spent one night at a motel in Salem, Alabama. Again, the people are very nice.

The last ten miles I rode in Alabama on a nice bike path. My phone rings. I stop the bike and answer the phone. It was Jimmy Carter's personal secretary. She informed me that the only time I could get close to him would be in church. Any other time, I had to make an appointment through the Carter Center, and it would be six to eight weeks before I could see him. I thanked her for calling and for giving me that information.

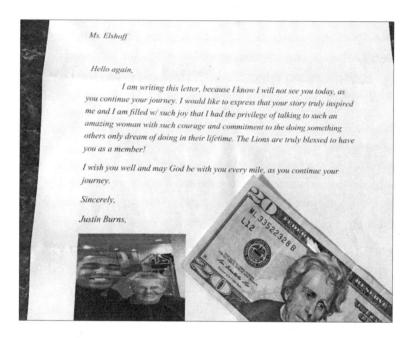

I thought I found the bad guy, but I guess I was wrong. He only looked bad.

These are Dan's, my son-in-law's, parents. Helga and John Day from Milwaukee. They stayed in the wintertime in the panhandle of Florida. I visited them, and I had a very very good time with them.

This guy I met at the pheasant shoot in Georgia.

This was the Lions Club in Georgia. The lady with the purple shirt is Alice.
She was instrumental in getting me together with president Jimmy Carter.

I never met many Toastmasters, but in North Carolina I met this Toastmaster and was invited to a Toastmasters club. Thanks to Mike for finding Toastmasters for me.

Georgia

The roads I traveled in Georgia

Monday, November 23, 2015

I entered Georgia somewhere near Columbus. I got on a bike trail and, as I peddled along, I met a policeman riding a bike. He stopped and we visited. His wife was from Germany. All along the trail people would show me signs that they liked my bike, or they would stop and ask questions.

I am on my way to Angela's house in Midland, Georgia. She is a member of the Columbus Lions Club and she will be my host while I am here. I finally got to Angela's house, however, I went past her house several times. She finally came out and stood on the street.

Angela Hollis and her husband, Tim, had a wonderful supper for me. She had invited the Columbus Lions club to her house to meet me. One person showed up. That was totally okay with me. I tell you what, Alice Stagg, one of the Lions members, turned out to be one of the main characters in this story. I told the Lions about my dream to see Jimmy Carter. Alice spoke up and said the she has a cousin in Plains, Georgia that played with Jimmy Carter's sister. She said that she would see what she could do about getting me to see Jimmy.

It was two days before THANKSGIVING. I didn't feel like being under foot with strangers on THANKSGIVING day. Besides, I had to be in Minnesota to speak at our District's Lions Midwinter convention in January. I decided I would rent a car the next day and drive home. I asked Angela if I could leave my ELF at their house. That was okay with her and Tim.

Tuesday, November 24, 2015

In the morning, Angela took me to the airport, and we got a car. We went back to her house. A guy that Angela knew worked at the TV station. Angela had told him about me, and he came to interview me. I saw the interview on my phone, and I have to say, that was a good interview. I loaded up all the stuff from my bike that I needed to take with me, and I proceeded on my drive home to Minnesota.

I left at about at three in the afternoon after all of the goodbyes. As I usually do, I drove around in circles for a while before I got on the right Interstate. At midnight, I got tired. It was raining cats and dogs. I started driving again after four hours of sleep. The weather had settled down a little bit. I had to change highways now and then. When I got into Iowa, or somewhere thereabout, I was welcomed with snow. Every once in a while, I stopped to take a nap.

Thursday, November 26, 2015. THANKSGIVING DAY

Early in the morning, I made it home. It was good to see everybody again.

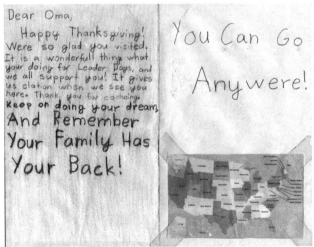

Homemade birthday card from my family.

Two weeks after I got home, I got a call from Alice in Georgia. She gave me two phone numbers for her cousin, Arleen Haugabook in Plains, Georgia. Alice said, "You give her a call right away." I did and Arleen said she would see what she could do to get me to see Jimmy Carter. A few days later, Arleen called me back and said, "Good news. I saw them (Jimmy and Rosalynn) at a funeral and I told them about you. In unison they said, 'We heard about her.'" Jimmy said, "You find out when she will be back from Minnesota, and we will come to your house for dinner."

The Midwinter Convention was to be held January 22-24, 2016. I was to talk on Saturday, the 23rd. I called Arleen and told her that I could be there on Sunday, January 31. My son-in-law, Dan got a plane ticket for me to fly from Rochester, Minnesota to Columbus, Georgia on Thursday, January 28th. I arrived in Columbus at about 2 pm. Angela and Tim, picked me up at the airport. Alice borrowed a trailer from a friend and picked the ELF and me up the next day. Her husband insisted on me not riding the bike to Plains. He said there was nowhere to stay in-between.

The Hallises, Arleen and C.G., did so, so much for me. I always feel like a simple thank is not enough. I feel like the little drummer boy in the Christmas story. Actually, less than that, I can't even make music.

As I am writing this book, I shed a lot of tears of gratitude and appreciation. I think, 'thank GOD I don't write on paper. It would be a total mess.'

Sunday, January 31, 2016

Alice and I stayed overnight at Arlene and C.G.'s house. C.G., Arleen's husband, likes to video tape everything. He and Arleen went ahead of me in the car to the church. I left with my ELF at 8:30 am. It was only a mile or two to the church. It was the most beautiful spring morning I ever remember. I was as calm as a cucumber until I got in the driveway of the church. A tall, wide-shouldered man came out of an SUV and walked toward me with his big German Shepherd. He said to me, "Get out of the bike." I suddenly forgot being calm. I got beyond nervous. I was almost shaking in my shoes. The dog checked me out and then went to the bike. After everything was okay, the officer told me to park the bike. C.G. stood there with his camera paraphernalia. Next to him stood his wife and Alice. They told me to park the bike next to the VIP's vehicles. I did that. I have never been the same since that day.

After that, we went into the church. The main entrance was guarded by secret service man. We had to go around the back. I felt like we were at the airport. They checked everybody's purse and used a wand on everyone but us. Someone called my name. "Hanna, you and your group come with me." They had the second row reserved for us. C.G. had to leave his camera stuff somewhere before he came into the church.

Then came the briefing. A rather humorous lady told us what to do and what not to do. She said that President Carter doesn't like applause. Also, when he comes in, we are to stay seated. She entertained and educated us for about one hour. Then Jimmy Carter came in for the Sunday School lesson. I don't remember what he talked about. I just kept watching the secret service guy standing by the door. That reminded me of WWII, when they had a Nazi standing near the altar. The person standing near the altar in WWII was for a totally different reason; the Nazi was to make sure that the minister didn't say anything against Nazi's.

Jimmy Carter did a very great job. And to think he had been at death's door a few months before. One of his grandsons had died at the age of 28 about a month earlier. President Carter is an amazing human being.

Then came the church service. It was excellent, but I don't remember anything from that, either.

Everyone left the church, except the people that wanted to have their picture taken with Jimmy Carter and his wife, Rosalynn. (They were married in 1946.)

We went back to Arleen and C.G's house. That was interesting. When we got there, two of the secret service vehicles were already sitting on the side of the street. Arleen, C.G. and Alice were already home when I got there. One of the secret service men asked Arlene how many people were invited. She wasn't sure; it kept changing. I don't know what they finally came up with. My nerves were wound up so tight like a two-dollar watch. My state of serenity from the early morning went out the window. I talked to one of the secret service guys sitting in the car. He was very nice. He asked about my bike, where I came from and a bunch of other questions. I finally was called to the house. It wasn't long af-

THE WHITE HOUSE
WASHINGTON

Dear Fellow Citizen:

There are certain unforgettable moments in everyone's life -- moments that we treasure as long as we live. I hope that for you this is one of them. It is my pleasure to welcome you most warmly to citizenship in the United States of America.

Our country stands for different things to different people. It is remarkable for its size, its beauty, and its natural and economic wealth. But what really makes it unique is the experiment of freedom that was begun here by the earliest settlers -- people who, like you, chose to come to these shores to begin a new life of liberty, challenge and opportunity.

The American experiment goes on. You are now a vital part of it.

As you share the rights and benefits of citizenship with your fellow Americans, I hope the knowledge that you are now a vital part of the Nation that Abraham Lincoln once called "the last, best hope of earth" will always be a source of pride to you.

Congratulations and best wishes.

Jimmy Carter
Gerald R. Ford

ter that, that the car came with the President. We all waited in the living room. The coffee table was covered with stuff that Jimmy Carter was supposed to sign. The most important thing on the table was a letter that I had received in 1977 when I got my citizenship. When I received

Dinner with the president Carter at my new host's, Haugabooks, house in Plains, Georgia. Willie Cooper is on the left, and Hanna Flynn is on the right.

The president, his wife, and myself

the letter, I read it. I got to the bottom of it expecting Jimmy Carter's signature, but instead it was Gerald Ford's, the previous president. That was why it was important for me to get Jimmy Carter's signature above Gerald Ford's. I don't know if everybody else noticed it, but I did.

Jimmy and Roselynn were seated on the couch by the window. Willie Cooper and his wife were sitting on chairs in the doorway, as was Alice. Hannah Flynn and Arleen were sitting in stuffed chairs. C.G. was behind me in a doorway with his camera stand. And I, I was standing, swinging my arms and telling my story. All that on tape. I acted like a monkey. I won't let anybody see that tape. I wish I could do that scene over.

Then, it was time to eat. Arleen's two daughters and granddaughter were working in the kitchen and serving the food. Arleen had the table set with placecards with our names telling us where we were to be seated. She had me at the head of the table and Jimmy Carter to my left and next to him, Rosalynn. I was trying to be quiet, but Arleen kept prompting me to talk about my cemetery lot and other stories.

Many thanks again to Alice Stagg, who got all of that in motion and a huge thank you to Arleen. By the way, I don't think that I mentioned that she was, at that time, 86 years young and she hopped around like a young filly.

THANKS TO EVERYONE THAT WAS INVOLVED IN MAKING MY DREAM COME TRUE!!!!!!

Monday, February 1, 2016

The weather is great here in Plains, Georgia. Alice is still trailering my ELF around. We are going to Americus, GA. We stopped in a town between Plains and Americus and met some Lions. I don't remember the name of the town. Alice and I are meeting my new hosts, Lewis and Mary Overholt, at a shopping center. We met Arlene from Plains, Georgia there, as well. We unloaded my ELF.

Oh, boy, the goodbyes get harder and harder!

Lion Willie Cooper had made the arrangements for me to stay with the Overholts. They are not Lions, but Lewis works with Willie Cooper at the food shelf. Lewis and Mary worked in Berlin, Germany as missionaries for 27 years. They speak perfect German.

The Overholts escorted me to their house where we had a wonderful visit and food.

Tuesday, February 2, 2016

Lewis Overholt talked me into trailering my ELF to Albany, GA. I stayed with Past International President Jim and Sharon Ervin. It was lucky that Lewis talked me into trailing my bike, because, around noon, it really started pouring. Light rain is not a problem, but heavy rain is not much fun.

I stayed two nights in Albany. They showed me around town. It was all great.

Friday, February 5, 2016

Jim escorted me out of town. He got to see what happens when I stop anywhere; two pickups stopped to inquire about the ELF. Jim talked to them and invited them to Lions.

I rode on to Camilla, Geoergia. Lots of time to Daydream.

 ### *End of My Marriage*

I wasn't going to tell you about myself or my failed marriage. But I decided to, because it might be some help to somebody.

Before I got married, my husband told me about how abusive his father was to him and the rest of his family. He said to me, "Don't ever let me become that way." That should have been the first sign. I learned that that doesn't work. Perhaps at first, it worked, but then, after a while, he would say, "I never said for you not to let me become that way." Then, he would say, "Prove it." It was my word against his.

My opinion, now that I am old, is that no one can change anybody else. One can be supportive, but that is all. The only person one can change is oneself.

Things got worse very, very slowly. He locked me out in the cold one night. After hours, I figured out a way to get back into the house. I never would mention it to our friends or anyone. I kept it from the kids.

One can sit in warm water very comfortably. You can add hot water very, very slowly. One doesn't notice that one is getting burned until it gets so bad, that one finally knows that they have to make a change or die.

After he locked me out, I thought I needed to make some changes. Divorce was out of the question. That happens in other families, but not in ours. In order for me to handle all the pain, I thought to myself, 'I am going to become an alcoholic.' I started with a fifth of Apricot brandy the next morning after he went to work. By noon, I looked in the mirror and said to myself, 'that is the dumbest thing you ever thought of.' I learned from that experiment that you either have the genetics to be an alcoholic or not. Luckily, I don't, or I would be drinking.

It reminds me of actress Carol Burnett. Both of her parents were severe alcoholics. She was raised by her grandmother in a one-room apartment. In the tabloids, it was written that Carol was so drunk that they had to drag her out of a restaurant. She sued the tabloids for personal slander, because she never in her life had drank even one drop of alcohol. She knows that there is a good chance that she inherited that gene. Once you get started drinking, you can't stop.

The second thing I seriously contemplated was suicide. Sounds very serious and it was. I had pretty healthy parents and my psychological health was in good enough shape that I felt I could get through that horrible thought.

I don't read the bible much, but I opened my little German bible. Just opened it and, strangely enough, on the right side of the page I open it to said that you can get a divorce but don't get remarried. I don't know where I saw that, but I have asked scholars of the bible and they tell me that it

is in the bible and where. I can never remember where they said it is, but that gave me permission to get a divorce and I did.

It all was a long time ago. I have some hard years behind me, but I survived, and I am Happy!

Back to my journey….

Past District Governor Lion Jack Taylor and his wife, Past District Governor Lion Georgia Taylor came in there sometime. Jack asked where I wanted to go. I said, "I know where I don't want to go. I don't want to go north, and I don't want to go into mountains. You can send me anywhere else." He called me almost every day. I could hear Georgia in the background saying, "Don't call her so much." I said, "That's okay. I hardly get any calls at all." Between Jack and his wife, Georgia, and Alice Stagg, they took care of me all the way through Georgia. I never had to pay for a hotel room. There was always someone waiting for me.

In Camilla, Georgia, I stayed with a Lion at a B&B.

Saturday, February 6, 2016

The Lions club was hosting a pheasant shoot. I couldn't figure out what was going to happen. They told me there would be lots and lots of hunters. I thought to myself, 'there must be a huge area to have that many hunters.' My hostess took me to the farm where the pheasant shoot took place.

I found out how it works. First of all, it is a big fundraiser for the Lions club. The hunters pay quite a bit of money to participate in the shoot. The turkeys are raised on a farm, because it gets too hot for them to live in the wild. They bring them in cages, which they set in a row behind a row of 10 huge round straw bales. The pheasants are let loose and the shooting starts. I think everybody gets to take one pheasant home. I am not sure how correct all of that is, but it goes something like that. The club members provide the meals. It was great fun.

Sunday, February 7, 2016

PDG Lion Jack Taylor escorted me to Michelle and Mike Miller's. I went to a Lions meeting. I don't recall what happened from then on until next Saturday.

Saturday, February 13, 2016. Into Florida.

I stayed overnight at Scott O'Brian in Florida.

Sunday, February 14, 2016

On my way to Blountstown, Florida, I saw a church that said, "Visitors Welcome." People were just walking in. I thought to myself, 'I am being called to go to church.' I did. However, the preacher kept on talking and talking, so I had to leave, or I would not have enough time to get where I had to go before dark. I left my donation and started to pedal my bike toward Blountstown. I found a very interesting motel. I mean VERY interesting. I was a little bit worried, but there was nowhere else to stay in that town. It was early evening. After I got my room, I rode around on my bike. I saw a woman with a kid at a gate talking to horses and a guy on the other side of the gate. I stopped to ask them about a restaurant. Before I knew it, the man invited me into their house to meet his mother-in-law. I visited with her and his wife. Next thing, they invited me to stay overnight. Unfortunately, I had already paid for the so-called motel room. I said I would come for the next night.

As always, I got up very early and went to a restaurant for breakfast. I sat close to the kitchen with my back toward the street. My Elf was sitting in front of the restaurant on the sidewalk. I was finished eating. As I walked out, a bunch of guys at a round table started talking to me about that contraption sitting outside. I pulled up a chair and started visiting. Some guy came in and delivered ammunition to a guy sitting next to me. We started discussing guns. I told them that I didn't like guns and that I didn't need one. The guy with the ammunition said to me, "What if someone comes up to you and holds a gun to your head?" "Well," I said, "I have my rubber ducky." I pulled a rubber ducky out of my pocket. I said, "When they see that, they have to laugh so hard that they forget what they were going to do with their gun." Of course, everyone had a good healthy laugh.

When I said I was going to Wewahitchka the next day, one other guy at the table spoke up. He said, "You can stay with my son and his wife." I told him he better call his son and asked him and his wife if that would be okay. He immediately did that, and they said it would be fine. That was great. He gave me their phone number and address.

It always feels exceptionally good when I have a place to stay instead of having to look for a motel. Although, the motel keepers have also been very generous and gracious.

I went to Gary and Delores's, the couple and mother I had told I would return to stay the next night. I had a great day with them. The next morning, I took off to Wewahitchka to meet my next host.

Tuesday, February 16, 2016

I am on my way to Wewahitchka, Florida. I still don't know how to say that town. I say whatchamacallit it. I had received a call from my son-in-law's parents, Helga and Jon. They were vacationing in Port St. Joe, Florida, which is near Wewahitchka. They invited me to come and see them there. It is less than 30 miles away. Again, a lonely road gives me lots of time to daydream.

 Caring for Caleb and Greta

There is so much to think about. I am thinking about when Caleb and Greta were little. I had so much fun with them and I hope they had fun, too. I think they did. We had a little table and I put little aprons on them, and we baked yeast bread. That was a lot of fun. We kind of trashed their mother's kitchen. At three in the afternoon was clean-up time. When their parents got home, everything was cleaned up, but they smelled the fresh baked bread. It was like in the CAT IN THE HAT story. The mother came

home and asked the kids, "What did you do?" and the kids answered, "NOTHING."

Caleb was the oldest and Greta was three years younger. As they got older and I took them to school, I always told them stories in the car. Once in a while, it would be quiet, and one of them, usually Greta, would say, "Tell us some stories."

We went for a lot of walks and met a few neighbors and their children. We met Donna Knipfer and her two children, April and Nick. After several years went by and April was in her last year of High School, she had to interview a person about a war. I told her that I could tell her a lot of stories, but they are after WWll. She interviewed me and did a tremendous job. She made a wonderful book out of the story. A few years later, Donna brought that book and gave it to me. It was hard for me to hold back my tears.

In the book was a poem April had written about me. I have permission to share that with you.

> *Thank You God for the Allies*
> *It all happened on June the 6th, of 1944*
> *D-Day was the beginning of the end of the war.*
> *It's a day we'll never forget*
> *Because Hitler wasn't such a threat.*
>
> *The Americans landed and fought the resistance,*
> *While other Allies offered assistance,*
> *We knew they could make the distance,*
> *They fought until Victory in Europe Day.*
>
> *They marched day in and day out,*
> *Liberated the camps with the Jews devout,*
> *We never even had a doubt,*
> *And on VE-Day, boy did we shout!*

So thank God for the Allies
Who saved our lives
The brave soldiers put their life on the line
Just so they could save mine

BY APRIL KNIPFER

FLORIDA

I arrived in Wewahitchka, Florida, at about one in the afternoon. I drove around town. I went in the grocery store. One lady talked to me. I asked her if she knew Brad and Michelle Bailey. She did and she told me where they lived. It was too early for me to go there. I got a sandwich and some chips at the grocery store. I went somewhere on the side of the street and ate my sandwich. My phone rang. It was my host, Michelle. She said, "People tell me that you are in town. Just come to the house. We live right on Highway 22 Number 3844. It is easy to find." I took right off. It was a few miles away. I got to their beautiful house. As I entered the house, in the huge foyer stood seven children in a half-circle all about four years old looking at me with their shiny eyes. It was incredibly cute. I will always have that picture in my mind and heart. I had the most wonderful time. In the evening, we went to a baseball game, which their son played in. I usually cheer at the wrong time, but it is good for a laugh.

Wednesday, February 17, 2016

Now I will go to Port St. Joe to visit Helga and Jon. Somehow, I was invited, or I found out that there was a Lions meeting in Port St. Joe at noon that day. I was there in plenty of time. There was standing room only. I gave the president my 'letter to the editor' telling how the Americans saved my life to read to the club. I can't read it. I get too emotional. I didn't think it would bother anybody else. I guess I was wrong.

When I looked around the corner, there were Helga and Jon having lunch. I was so excited to see them. I didn't expect them to be there. It was great.

I followed them a little way, then stopped and left my Elf with one of the Lions members. I stayed four days with Helga and Jon. We had a wonderful visit. The last day I picked up my bike and rode it back to town. We left the ELF by the police station.

Jon took me to the newspaper office. They were excited to interview me.

Sunday, February 21, 2016

Helga and Jon took me back to my bike at the police station. I was going back to whatchamacallit (Wewahitchka) to Brad and Michelle's. If I make it there by 10 am, I will get there in time for church. I did and it was great.

In the afternoon, they had a get-together at Brad's father's place in the woods. He was the guy I met in the restaurant in Blountstown. He had a big shed set up with sleeping quarters and a kitchen facility. We had a wonderful afternoon.

In the evening we went back to Wewahitchka to their house.

Monday, February 22, 2016

Another hard goodbye. This time, I am not coming back. Now back to Blountstown to Gary and Delores house.

I am riding on lots of lonely roads with lots of time to think some more.

 More Caleb and Greta/My Childhood in Germany

I got to know Jon and Lori's neighbors' nanny, Jeanie. They had a boy and a girl a little older than Caleb and Greta. The six of us spent time together. I told them the popcorn story. One day I said, "Let's just do like we did it in Germany and not put a lid on it." Jeanie literally fell off her stool, she laughed so hard. The kids, also, were laughing and laughing. Then it would be quiet and then another kernel would pop and we would all laugh again. It was a little bit of a job to clean up the grease that splattered all over the stove, but it was worth it.

If you need a good laugh in your house sometime, give that a try.

Another time, when Jeanie and the kids were over, there was a snake curled up in the dining room area. Jeanie said, "If I didn't know any better, I would think that snake is real." About that time, the snake started moving. There was a lot of screaming. It was just a bull snake. I put it out in the garden. It was a pretty big one. I am not fond of snakes, but I am not that afraid of them, as long as it is not a rattlesnake.

All of that thinking led me to my own childhood. I was four or five. We didn't have a radio, but our neighbors, the Behnkes had one. They had a bigger farm and a nicer and bigger house. Theirs was the second house built in the village. I don't know if you remember, but the farms are side by side in the villages in Germany.

I must have wandered over there with my brothers one day and heard people talking in that box. I asked, "When do those people in the box eat?" I was told that, after I leave, they will give them something to eat. I was gullible then and not too smart. I always say, "I was born dumb and never learned anything."

I liked cats, and I still do. There were no toys after the war. I dressed the cats up in doll clothes. I gave them a bottle and fed them milk. They let me do anything I wanted to them.

I always wanted to be in a circus with my cats. In those days, that was the only entertainment. Once a year, the circus came and there was a horse show once a year, too. I loved the horse show and I went to that when I was about ten years old. In the evening, they had fireworks. I DIDN'T like that. It reminded me too much of the war. I was just a baby when the sirens went off and my family had to go to the basement. I think the subconscious mind causes the fear. When I heard the tornado siren the first time, I was very frightened, but it doesn't bother me anymore.

I arrived at Gary and Delores's house in Blountstown. They were glad to see me. They invited me to stay as long as I wanted.

Tuesday, February 23, 2016

Delores and Gary took me around town. They showed me an example of what towns used to look like. It was very interesting. In the afternoon, I wanted to go to the post office. I had to go across the river to Bristol. I did that with my bike. It was a nice little ride. The time changes once you cross the river, but my phone is very smart and keeps the proper time. I got to the post office and the library wasn't far from there. I needed some copies made of the papers I handed out to people at the gas stations and all the places I stopped.

At the library they put me in a special room to make the copies. I, also, looked in a phone book for a Lions club. Just as I was looking in the phone book, a tall gentleman walked in with a huge smile on his face. He asked, "Is that your bike with the Lions flag on it?" Then I had huge smile on my face. "Yes, it is. Are you a Lion?" "Yes, I am. My name is Joe Schuler." Well, we were friends right away. He told me that they had a meeting the next evening at the restaurant. Bob Pinkerton would pick me up. Oh, boy, how do those things always fall into place.

A lady came to the meeting a little bit late. She was not a Lion, but she had seen in some paper that I was going to be at that Lions meeting. She talked to me after the meeting and told me she would escort me to Quincy, Florida, the next day. I will stay with Debbie and Ronnie in Quincy. We decided to meet at that restaurant at 10 am.

Can you imagine all of that? By the way, her name is Sandra.

Wednesday, February 24, 2016

Sandra and I met at 10 am at the restaurant in Blountstown. It is only 32 miles to Quincy. It is nice to have someone escort me. We got to Debbie and Ronnie's at about one in the afternoon. Sandra and I will stay with them. Debbie had to open the gate for us. She was so happy to see us. She welcomed us literally with open arms. She said right away, "You can stay here as long as you want." That was quite the invitation. I stayed there three nights. It was a great experience. Debbie has a lot of education. I didn't really understand what she did in her younger years, but it had something to do with aquatics. She quit her job in order to take

[One of Us

Hanna Elshoff

Chatfield Lions Club, Minnesota

Growing up in a small German village, Hanna Elshoff dreamed of coming to America. Now, the 72-year-old grandmother is living her dream of riding a bike around the United States, including a stop to fulfill yet another dream—meeting a former U.S. president (and Lion) who inspired her to become a citizen.

| Was a nanny for 16 years | Owns a farm in Minnesota | Rides the solar- and pedal-hybrid "ELF" bike |

Elshoff stops at International Headquarters on her ELF bike.

A Free Spirit

I always felt that I needed more elbow room than my small community in Germany allowed. I arrived here speaking no English at 18. I rode my bike everywhere, and I wanted to ride through the U.S. But I knew I had to be footloose and fancy-free before I could do it.

Living Courageously

I had a stroke six years ago while giving a speech at a Toastmasters competition. I remember thinking I was going to die, and I was at peace with it. Ten days later I walked out of the hospital. I thought, I wasn't kept alive for nothing. I became determined to go on this ride fearlessly.

Pedaling with Gratitude

Along with raising funds for Leader Dogs, meeting Lions and sharing my passion for Toastmasters, my mission on this ride is to thank veterans. My family found out after World War II that a neighbor was SS and had orders to send us away because we were members of the Free Lutheran Church. If the Americans hadn't come ... they saved our lives.

Journey to Georgia

Years ago, I saw a guy on TV saying he was a farmer and was running for president. My family were farmers and I thought, only in America could a farmer run for president. I became a citizen so I could vote for him. I didn't quite make it, but President Jimmy Carter has always held a special place in my heart. I have my letter welcoming me as a citizen—signed by President Gerald Ford—with me. I'm heading to Plains, Georgia, to try to get Carter to add his signature.

No Regrets

I was told my dream of this ride was quixotic. Thankfully I received the extra push I needed at the international convention in Hamburg, when International President Barry Palmer announced his theme, "Follow Your Dream." I'm riding with a purpose, meeting beautiful people everywhere and touching lives with my story. Every day I say, it can't get any better.

Follow Elshoff's ride, invite her to visit your club and find out if she fulfills her dream of getting Carter's autograph at "Hanna's Dream Ride" on Facebook.

 Digital LION
Watch a video about Elshoff's ride at lionmagazine.org.

Do you know a Lion who you think has a great story or deserves a bit of recognition? Email us a brief description of the Lion and the reason you're making the nomination to lionmagazine@lionsclubs.org. Please include "One of Us" in the subject line.

The article from the Lions magazine

care of her parents, who lived on the farm that Debbie inherited. What a beautiful farm with a creek running through it. Debbie, also, learned blacksmithing. She had a shop on the farm that, until a few years ago, had been an art studio.

BACK TO GEORGIA

Sunday, February 28, 2016

I could have stayed with Debbie and Ronnie longer, but I am like a gypsy, I have to keep moving. Sandra, Debbie and Ron escorted me to Cairo, Georgia. On the way we went through the very little town of Calvary. The only things there were a sign, a few houses, and a very nice Lions building. The first weekend in November, they have a huge festival, called MULE DAY. Jack Taylor told me that people come from everywhere. The pastures and fields are full of trailers and campers. They've held the festival for 40 years. About 30 to 40 thousand people show up for that. I told them I would try to come back for that.

When we got to Cairo, we found the Grady motel right outside of town. I stayed there.

Well, now it was time to say goodbye again. It is always the same story.

Monday, February 29, 2016

Arleen from Plains, Georgia has a brother that lives in Cairo. I had his phone number. I gave him a call. We met at a gas station. He escorted me to his house, and I stayed there overnight. I had the honor of sleeping in a room with a bedroom set from the Civil War.

February 29th is in here twice. You must find out how to correct that and the true time line.

Tuesday, March 1, 2016

Sarah and Ed fixed me a very beautiful, picturesque breakfast. It was great. I had contacted Jack Tayler to see where I should go from there. He sent me to Norman Park, Georgia.

I went on my way to Norman Park. I don't remember much about that place except when I got there, I saw the huge building. I was supposed to meet the maintenance manager, Lion Mike Arnold. I met a lot of the workers, because of my ELF, of course. I finally got together with Lion Mike. I had a whole lot of people around me.

It was a huge, huge building with lots of sleeping rooms. I understand that it had been the Georgia Baptist Conference Center. It was big.

Mike showed me the room I was going to use. It looked like I had the whole campus to myself. I rode my bike around and met a lot of people at the only restaurant in town. I took a lot of pictures of people and people took a lot of pictures of the ELF and me. I finally went back to my room. I think I was the only one left on that whole huge campus. I wasn't at all afraid. I never was afraid. With all the people that think about me and wish me safe travels and worry about me, there is no room left for me to be afraid. That's how I see it.

Tuesday, March 2, 2016

As usual, I got up early and went to the restaurant to have breakfast. There was more visiting and more picture taking. It was fun, like always.

I had directions from Jack to go to Tifton, Georgia. It was really nice of Jack to do all of that for me. I am on my way to Tifton.

Lots of time to daydream.

 Monkey Experiments

There is a story I would like to share with you. I saw it about 15 or so years ago on the Today Show. They did a study on monkeys. They wondered why a female monkey has female behavior and male monkey has male behavior. So, they injected an unborn female fetus with male hormones. That female monkey had male behavior. Then, they injected an unborn male monkey with female hormones. That monkey had female behavior.

Then, they did the same with a male and a female baby monkey after being born and there was no change in the behavior of those monkeys.

Nothing was said about homosexuality. My question is, "Could that have something to do with homosexuality in humans?" I think most people know that a woman gives off both female and male hormones. When my daughter was born, when I got her home from the hospital, I noticed that she had breasts and a few days later she, also, had milk. I quickly took her to the doctor. He assured me that there was nothing to be concerned about, those were just leftover female hormones. Now, if she had been born a boy, would he have been homosexual? Makes one wonder.

My mother always said that I am not to judge. I am not inside that person. Lots to think about!

After stops at gas stations and McDonalds, I finally got to Tifton. I don't remember the name of the Lion I met in Tifton, but he took me to a Hampton Motel where I spent the night.

Wednesday, March 3, 2016

Jack sent me to a Lions camp in Douglas, GA that was run by Mike and Gail Williams. When I first got there, I couldn't find anybody to check in with. Adult people walked around but they didn't look at me or say anything to me. It was kind of strange. I finally went to one of the houses and a lady answered. It was Gail. I was happy. She told me that they had a group at the camp that had been there for a week or so, and they don't talk to anybody outside of their group or to each other. I understood that they were from different churches. By Sunday, they were gone. Mike told me that they have been coming there for several years. He said that they have been good to the camp.

Mike and Gail are just tremendous caretakers. They have done so much for the camp over the years and they did a lot for me.

Thursday, March 4, 2016

I am not going to mention every town that I stopped in, but I was always welcomed and treated like royalty. I can't say enough good things about the American people. All of them, from my experience, have been just great.

I am going to jump to Lions Debbie and Larry Grigger in Lyons, Georgia. They met me in a town before Lyons and escorted me to their house. Larry has a drone and took many pictures with it from above. I don't know what all to tell you about them. They are a very lively couple. Larry had started writing a book about his uncle that wanted a car that someone was driving so he just shot him. He had quite a bit written. He said he would finish it someday. I told him, "Set a date. Someday never comes. If you don't make it by that date, then set another date." Many years ago, I set a date to begin this journey that I am on. I thought I had to wait until I was eighty. At my 70th birthday party, I decided that I can do it when I am 75 years old. I had joined the Lions and every town has a Lions club. I can use that to my advantage. That gave me five years to make my plan. I read somewhere that when you make plans, life sends you in a totally different direction. And that happened to me.

Larry and Debbie did so much for me. They set up an interview for me with a lady from the region's magazine. They gave me the magazine later. I put it in a very special place. Well, it is so special that I can't find it.

Friday, March 11, 2016

I am on my way to Statesboro, GA to a Lions convention. That night, I stayed at the Comfort Inn, which the local District Governor had arranged for me. Thank you, again, Hannah.

Sunday, March 13, 2016

I left Statesboro and went to Sylvania, Georgia. After that, I was told by Jack Tayler to go to Brunson, South Carolina. He gave me a contact name and number.

Again, I was on lonely roads.

Mansions Along the Road

I am thinking about a road, a long strip of highway on this journey, that impressed me. I don't remember which state it was in. All I remember is that I was on that road for several hours.

I passed enormous houses with at least an acre, maybe two, of lawn around each house. Each house had a tall fence around it with a gate that was closed. I never saw anybody coming or going. Once in a while, a car would meet me or pass me. It was a strange neighborhood. I saw miles and more miles of those kinds of houses. I have to say, I feel sorry for the people that live there. I didn't plan on writing a book or I would have made note of which state I saw them in.

I finally arrived in Brunson, South Carolina!

9
Hanna's
Dream
Ride

South Carolina

The roads I traveled in South Carolina

Tuesday, March 15, 2016

I am now in Brunson, South Carolina. I was told that I could stay at the Lions clubhouse. I rode around and asked people where it was. I rode around quite a bit. I finally found it. I arrived at the same time as the people who lived across the road came home. They came right over to talk to me. I didn't even have time to call the guy that was to bring the key for the Lions clubhouse. I visited for a bit. Before I knew it, the lady invited me to her house to stay overnight. I guess that's why I rode around for a while, to meet up with the neighbors. Her name was Virginia. The guy with her was just a friend. He went home. Her husband had died a few years ago. All she had was a dog named Gizmo. I stayed there one night. The next day I went to Orangeburg and then to Camden, S.C.

The road from Orangeburg to Camden was very, very busy with mostly lumber trucks, but lots of other cars and trucks, too. The biggest problem was that there was no shoulder. Trees and bushes were right next to the road. Once in a while, there was a driveway for me use to get out of the way.

I don't know how Richard Pinkerton got a hold of me, but he had called me the day before and told me that I could stay at his house, and that he had a trailer that he could use to trailer my bike. I told him that I have no problem riding the bike. After about 15 miles, I stopped somewhere and sat in the woods and thought about it. It was downright dangerous to continue riding on that road with all that traffic. I called Richard and asked him if he could pick me up. I told him which road I was on and that the bike is sitting alongside of the road. I waited about an hour before Richard and his friend, Lion Jim Varn came and picked me up. I was very, very happy. By then, the traffic had let up a lot, but I was still glad.

I spent two nights at Richard and his family's house. It was great.

I rode my bike to Mc Bee, South Carolina. I don't recall how I got in touch with Lion Leon and Angela Stallings. Again, super people. They have a retired Greyhound; a nice, gentle and very tall dog. They have a huge fenced-in yard so that the dog can run.

Friday, March 18, 2016

I went to Lion Susan Redman's in Wallace, S.C. I listen to my GPS for the first time. I didn't really know where I was to go. The GPS told me that I had arrived at my destination. It took me to a kind of messy looking place. I knocked on the door. A gentleman came out, and I asked him if Susan Redman lived there. He said, "No," and he didn't know where she lived. I called her. She told me that someone was coming to find me. The guy found me about a few miles away from Susan's house. She had invited the Lions Club. We had supper and had a great time visiting.

North Carolina

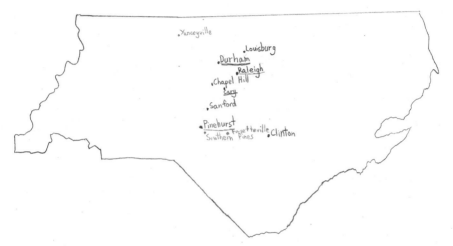

The roads I traveled in North Carolina

Tuesday, March 22, 2016

I am riding into North Carolina on Highway 1, a four-lane highway. I am going to Pinehurst. It was somewhat quiet with a nice wide shoulder. Suddenly, I saw a rather big turtle in the middle of the road. At that moment, I didn't see any traffic coming. I quickly got out of my bike. I picked the turtle up and carried him to the other side of the highway and into the woods. That was the first time I saw such a large turtle. I felt good; maybe I saved a life.

Later on, I stopped at a gas station in a wooded area. A man came out of the woods. He was looking through the garbage. I talked to him. He looked like he was homeless. We just exchanged words like, "The weather is nice," etc. I would have liked to help him some, like the turtle, pick him up and put him in a safe place, but that is not so easy to do to a person. It was kind of sad just to leave him behind.

I continued on Highway 1 until it came to an end. To get to Pinehurst, I had to go on a squiggly road. I called Lion Ron Kelly. I don't know how all those people found out about me, but they had called me to say that I could stay at their house. I felt like I might be lost. After many calls, I got ahold of Ron and he came and found me. Somehow, I had gotten myself high up on a pile of dirt. I have no idea how I got on that pile. They were working on building a big shopping center there. Ron called me, he could see me. I finally got off that dirt pile and found Ron. He escorted me to his house on a golf course. It was very, very nice. I met his wife, Jan. She was working in the front yard.

When Ron escorted me to his house, I was going downhill and the brakes on the ELF hardly worked. Thank goodness the traffic light turned green so that I could cross the highway without stopping.

I stayed there for Easter. I really had a good time. We had a beautiful Easter Dinner. I met the family. It was especially nice to meet Kathy, their daughter, from Chapel Hill, N.C. She invited me to her house.

Someone from the bike shop came out to fix the brakes on the bike. Ron also called the newspaper to interview me. That guy had just moved to town. I was his first victim.

Monday, March 28, 2016

Every morning Jan made a picture-perfect breakfast. She gets up any time after 5 am. Then she creates the food. Every day she makes something different. It was totally impressive.

Well, another goodbye. Every one is tough, but some are a little tougher. This is one of them. I will stop mentioning them, because it is always the same or similar. I feel you must get bored with the same rhetoric.

I am on my way to Sanford, North Carolina. I have a contact number and names, Roy and Billy Jernigan. I will stay with them.

Well, I went far, far out of my way, but it was a beautiful ride. I stopped and took pictures of cows and horses. The horses always run when they see the ELF, but the cows come to the fence and want to have a conversation. I tell them where I came from and all kinds of gobbledegoop. They always listen intently, but never tell me anything. Oh well, that's life.

My phone rings as I am conversing with my animal friends. It is Ron Kelly. "Where are you?" I tell him and he asked again. He couldn't figure it out. I was following the map. "If you know where you are going, I guess that's okay." he said. I was somewhat nervous. With my poor sense of direction and trouble with left and right, I need good luck.

About five in the evening, I was somewhere on the edge of a town. I saw a motel. I got a room there. I got into the room. I was just about make myself comfortable, when my phone rings. It was Roy Jernigan. "Where are you?" I am in a motel, but I don't know for sure where I am." I guess I am on the edge of Sanford. I didn't see a sign anywhere. "We were going to have you stay at our house." I had just checked in, but I can check back out. "I'll come and escort you to our house." I told him the name of the motel. He knew where that was. I went into the motel office and told him that I was leaving. I decided not to ask for the money back. I just left it.

In a half an hour, Roy showed up. I followed him. At first it was ok, but then we got on what seemed like an Interstate. It wasn't, but the traffic was horrendous. It was the busiest time in the evening. Then I remembered that Ron had checked to see if it was legal for me to ride on that highway. He checked with the police and they said it was okay. I was supposed to take that highway. It was a good thing I didn't ride on it by myself because it would have been scary. It was very scary now. Roy didn't really know how to escort me. If he would have put his flashers on and drove on the shoulder, perhaps it would have been better. I tried to get his attention to stop him. I finally got him to notice me flashing my lights on and off. He stopped on the side of the shoulder. I said, "I don't think I am supposed be on here. People are getting kind of mad and they are driving very fast." "We only have one more exit to go." So, he went on. Boy, I was so happy to get off that thing and get to their house. Roy told me that he didn't know how else to go. I said that, before they built that road, they had a road that would get you wherever you had to go. He hadn't thought of that. The next day, he showed me where the old road goes so that I could get out of there.

I had a wonderful stay at their house, which I been having at everybody's house. Billy is Roy's wife. I don't know if that is her real name. I never asked. She was a wonderful lady. She was working on a clergy stole for her son. It was very fine needlework. I used to have patience to do knitting and that kind of stuff, but not anymore. I just pedal my ELF.

After I left Sanford, I went to Chapel Hill, N.C. But first, I had to find my way out of Sanford. Wouldn't you know, I went on the on ramp of the highway I was on the day before. I had to turn around. That wasn't easy. There were cars coming one after the other, and there wasn't much room to turn around. The ELF has two wheels in front. It is hard to maneuver that beast. I was glad when I found the right place to go.

Now I have lots of time to daydream.

 Nestle's Quick

Everywhere I go, I get one complement after another. People say that I inspire them and all kinds of things like that. I am terribly humbled by all of those kind words. I say it's the ELF that draws attention, but they come back with, "The ELF didn't get anywhere by itself." I just don't know what to say, except "Thank you." It is very kind of everyone saying those kind words.

I am not a perfect person by any stretch of your imagination. I have done some naughty things in my lifetime. When I was a kid, I loved chocolate a whole lot. I remember that, after the war, we couldn't buy much, especially chocolate. At Christmas, we would get one chocolate bar. Of course, mine would be gone in one or two days. My sister, who is 6 years older, would save hers until it was nearly moldy. I helped her out and sneaked a little bit at a time.

The British or the Americans gave us Nestle's Quick. That was good stuff. My mother would hide it in the hutch in the Parlor. She, also, kept the cream in the hutch. We had a cream separator. She would save enough cream to make butter. I discovered that the cream and Nestle's Quick was a delicious combination. So did my brother, Hans, who is 7 years older than me. Neither one of us knew that the other was eating cream with Nestle's Quick. I don't know if my mother ever noticed it. She never said anything. She would hide candy somewhere and I would find it. After I ate it, I would tell her that I found candy and ask if I could have some. She would say, "Yes." I would say, "That is good, because I already ate it."

 Discipline in German Schools (In the 40s and 50s)

When I was in the first grade, we had Herr Freitag. He was not a nice guy. I guess none of the teachers were very nice in those days. We had the same teacher for eight grades. One time, Irmgard, my sister didn't raise her hand when she knew the answer to whatever the question was. Herr Freitag beat her with a stick across her back so bad that she was bleeding. That's when my dad got on the school board and they got rid of Herr Freitag. I remember they had a schoolboard meeting at our house. There were about six men in the parlor with the door closed. There was a room off the parlor. I thought I had to get something out of that room, but I was just nosy and needed an excuse to go through the parlor.

We got a new teacher, Herr (Mr.) Fahrenholz. He was better. I think I was in third grade and I didn't know the answer in math or something. He grabbed my right ear and slapped me on the left cheek. I had a nervous reaction and I smiled. Then, he grabbed my left ear and slapped the other cheek. When people would talk about that teachers don't have the right to touch a child, I would defend the children. There is no need to touch the children. There are other ways to deal with problems. Even to shame a child doesn't fix the problem. There are many other ways of discipline. At least, that is what I think. I learned a lot taking care of Caleb and Greta.

It never even crossed my mind to hit them. There are many ways to teach
without causing harm. Just, simply talk to them.

Wednesday, March 30, 2016

I am on my way to Chapel Hill. I am learning to use the GPS on my
phone. It tells me to take a left into a new housing development. I did.
Now I take a right, then another right. There was no road. I must have
made a mistake. I rode around and around. I always ended up at the
same spot where there was no road. It was Wednesday. My friend with
all the computer gadgets and knowledge has Wednesdays off. I'll give
him a call. It was about ten in the morning. I say, "Jon, tell me where I
am. I am lost." He gets his computer fired up and in no time, he knows
where I am. Then, he asked me which direction I am facing. Of course,
I had no idea. About that time, a pickup stopped beside me. The driver
wanted to know if I had problems. I said, "Yes, sir. Which way am I facing?" I briefly clued him in that I was talking to my friend in Rochester, Minnesota and that he was helping me out of my mess. The two figured out where I had to go. I had to go back on the main road and head
to Chapel Hill. You can't always trust the GPS.

I arrived in Chapel Hill at about three in the afternoon. I went in the
bar/restaurant and made lots of friends. It was surely a friendly city. If
I met people on the sidewalk, they would look up and greet me. I really liked it there.

Later on, Joe, Kathy's husband, met me, and we went to their town-
house. I think they lived on the third story. I think the garage was underground. I can't really remember. Joe had many regular bikes. Kathy
was kind enough to drive to Cary and show me exactly how I had to go
to get to Wendy's house. She warned me that that road is very busy on
weekdays and to be very careful.

Sunday, April 3, 2016

I was neighbors of Tiemann's when Wendy was a little girl. She met
a guy at IBM in Rochester. They got married and were transferred to

Cary, North Carolina. I am going to Wendy's house in Cary, N.C. The road was very quiet, because it was a Sunday. Since I knew where I was going, it was a great ride. I had never met Wendy's husband, Bob. He was mowing the lawn when I arrived. I met their two daughters and, of course, Wendy. I hadn't seen her for many, many years. It was great. I stayed there two nights.

Tuesday, April 5, 2016

In the morning, I was just tootling around the neighborhood, when my phone rang. It was someone from Organic Transit in Durham, N.C. where the ELF was made. "Where are you?" "I am just riding around." was my response. "We are having a party for you and invited a bunch of people." I didn't know that. "When is that going to happen?" "About four this afternoon." I went to Wendy's and packed all my stuff and took off for Durham. If everything went okay, I could make it to Durham in time for the party. I was going on the Tobacco Trail. The first obstacle I met was men working on a bridge. By hook and crook, I got around that. It took me quite a while. Then I found the trail. Now I have clear sailing, I thought. Well, they had barricades every few miles. The first one I got around by going through the trees and bushes. The second one, there was no way I could get around it. I called Organic Transit and told them they had to come and get me. Rob Cotter, the inventor of the ELF, came and got me. I hadn't gotten very far. Oh boy, I felt bad, but Rob is a very cool, kind guy. We got there a little late, but it had to be okay. I had to give a little talk. If I remember correctly, I did a lousy job.

I stayed three nights in their office. I got out my air mattress and sleeping bag. At 6 pm, they were all gone. They locked the doors and I was all by myself. It was great. At five in the morning, I rolled up everything and put it out of the way. During the day, I walked around in Durham. One morning, I sat on a bench and was working on my Facebook page, when, across the highway, I saw a guy sleeping on a bench. I kept looking up. Once-in-a-while, he would sit up and then he would lie down again. Finally, he just sat there. I went over to him and started talking to him. He told me that he had an appointment at the Methodist church to find him a place to live. His appointment was at 10 am. At about 9:30, he started walking. I asked him if I could walk with him. He was okay with that. He was a pretty nice guy. His wife kicked him out of the house because he was drinking. He was homeless. We walked through a park where there were a couple of guys setting up cameras and that kind of stuff. I talked to them. The homeless guy kept on walking. I tried to catch up with him, but I never saw him again.

One of the days, I walked past an office building. Suddenly, a guy came running out and said to me, "Do you remember me? I met you at the coffee shop in Cary." I remembered him very well. We talked about my ELF. Yes, that ELF is a conversation piece.

The guy I met at the coffee shop in Cary, and here he is in Durham.

Friday, April 8, 2016

At 5 am, Rob Cotter took me to Raleigh, N.C. to the Airport. I left the ELF with Organic Transit. I had to be in Minnesota for our Lions Multiple Convention. I was to speak at the convention on the 23rd of April. That is a big convention. It covers all of Minnesota, Manitoba and North West Ontario.

I don't remember much from being in Minnesota. The time went fast. I spent a few days at home. I talked to Jan and told her that I had lost a Lions flag again. She said to get enough material for two flags. We should have done that in the first place. I didn't lose a flag after that.

Wednesday, May 4, 2016

I returned to North Carolina. Wendy picked me up at the Raleigh Airport. She had a very busy day. That afternoon, she had to pick up one of her daughters, Sarah, at the Airport. Sarah and her husband had been living in Austria for several years. They were going to move back to the USA and Sarah had to find a house to live in. That is a big job.

Wendy is extremely calm. None of that bothered her. At least, she didn't show it. It is a nice feature to have.

Friday, May 6, 2016

I don't remember who took me to Durham to pick up my bike. I think Bob took me on his way to work. They really did a lot of work on that bike. They reinforced one side where the fiberglass had broken. I had Duct tape everywhere. Fiberglass is easy to repair. I don't know what all they did, but I know they did a lot. There was no charge. That was really great. I rode the ELF back to Wendy's. Too bad I can't ride on the Tobacco Trail. That would have been so easy.

I got back at about 4 pm. Kathy from Chapel Hill picked me up at 7 pm to take me to, I thought she said, camping at Lake Norman . It was a far cry from camping. It was a beautiful, huge house that was only used for weekends. Joe was good friends with the people that owned it. We were the only ones that were there. The next day, Kathy's parents came. I have never seen such a house. They even had a complete bar room. I can't describe it to do it justice.

We had a wonderful time. We went on a pontoon ride on the lake to Lions Camp Dogwood. It's a beautiful camp. We got a great tour of the camp.

Monday, May 9, 2016

On Monday, they took me back to Wendy's. I stayed at Wendy's two more days, and then I left. I was going to Washington D.C. and then to New York.

Thursday, May 12, 2016

The decision was made to go to Organic Transit in Durham. I thought I would say, "Hi and goodbye." I got there about noon. "Where are you heading?" one of the salesmen asked. That question came up many times. "I don't know." was the comment come back from me. David, one of the salesmen got a map out and we looked at it. I always looked at the size of the black circle next to the city name, thinking they would have a motel. I was looking north of Durham. David said there is not a city with a motel anywhere in that area. Then David said, "A few weeks ago, there were a couple older men here looking at the ELF. One of the guys, Sam, was 91 years old. The other one was probably in his sixties. They were leaving Saturday to go to Washington DC with a group. They meet at the bell tower at the University in Raleigh. Maybe this coming Saturday you can meet them there."

Dave made phone calls, but couldn't get a hold of anybody. He told me to just go there at 8 am. He was sure I could ride with them. Dave also made reservations for me at one of the airport motels for the night. I thanked him and took off. At about 4 pm I arrived at the airport motel. It was kind of tricky to get to that particular motel. I finally made it.

Friday, May 13, 2016

In the morning, I walked around to figure out how to get out of there. In the process, I visited with people. I talked to a pilot and other significant people. My bike was parked next to a pickup. The guy was just about to leave. Well, he asked me about the bike. In conversation, he was telling me that his son had died a few months ago. I asked him how that happened. "He had an argument with his girlfriend, so he shot himself. I sold every one of my guns." that guy told me.

I finally took off from the motel. It was a bit tricky, but I made it. I am on my way to the University in Raleigh. I got there at about one in the afternoon. I scoped out the area. I found a motel, checked in and then rode around a little bit again.

Saturday, May 14, 2016

I got up very early. I checked out at 6 am. I rode to the bell tower and looked around. The bell tower is covered with wonderful sayings on copper plaques and lots of beautiful pictures.

It got close to 8 am. A few people showed up. I asked them If they were from the Veterans for Peace group that rides with Sam to Washing D.C. They were. I asked them if I could ride along and what it would cost. It costs fifty dollars, but we had to wait for the lady that takes the money. There was quite the commotion before ev-

One of many sayings on the bell tower in Raleigh.

erybody got there. There was a group of elderly ladies that had written a couple of songs for the send-off.

This is one of the songs:

Song for Sam, Lyrics by Vicki Ryder

We love you Sam, Oh, yes, we do,
We hope you can get the message through:
When the US goes to war, we're blue
Oh, Sam, we love you!

We hope you have a good productive ride,
And tell them that too many now have died
Just for some corporate greed and pride,
Oh, Sam, we love you!

We should have learned it in Vietnam,
That making war's a really stupid plan,
We've got to stop them if we can.
We're counting on you, Sam!

We've seen enough of killing and of war,
We want our taxes spent to help the poor.
So, go and tell 'em, Sam, to war no more
Oh, Sam, we love you!

This is another…:

THE WAR ECONOMY, Lyrics by Vicki Ryder (tune: "99 Bottles of Beer on the Wall")

They tell us there's no money for jobs or health care plans,
But there's always plenty of it to make war in far off lands.
We spend it all for war and not for schools or jobs, that's true.
So, how's this war economy workin' out for you?
The answer is that profiteers make money off these wars,
They buy the votes of Congress….. and keep on makin' more.
They fund the corporations while the rest of us get screwed.
So, how's this war economy workin' for you?
So go and tell 'em , Sam and all, these wars have got to end!
There are better ways for us our nation to defend.
Schools and healthcare, jobs, clean water ….. those are things we need
To keep us strong and keep us safe from rampant corporate greed.
We're biking off to Washington and raging strong today;
We're singin' truth to power, growin' stronger every day.
We've paid our dues, we've fought and died ; it's time to say NO
    MORE!
WE DEMAND A PEACEFUL ECONOMY…….we won't pay for war!

Jimmy Carter spoke the following about war at the end of his ceremony in Oslo, Norway, where he received the Nobel Prize for Peace on December 10, 2002.

"Ladies and gentlemen:

War may sometimes be a necessary evil. But no matter how necessary, it is always evil, never a good. We will not learn how to live together in peace by killing each other's children.

The bond of our common humanity is stronger than the divisiveness of our fears and prejudices. God gives us the capacity for choice. We can choose to alleviate suffering. We can choose to work together for peace. We can make these changes – and we must.

Thank you."

The first day, we rode only 40 miles because we didn't really get started until 10 am. It was quite different then riding by myself. It was kind of nice. I didn't have to figure out where we were going. I just followed along. A few cars and pickups went ahead of us. At about 1 pm, we stopped for lunch. They had everything prepared. This was the seventh trip they had made. We had a nice lunch. After we rested a little, we went on to Louisburg, N.C. I don't remember were we stayed in Louisburg.

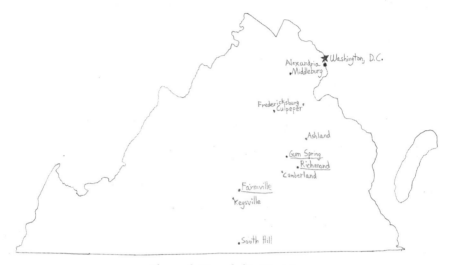

The roads I traveled in Virginia

Sunday, May 15, 2016

The next day we rode 60 miles. We stayed in South Hill, Virginia. I didn't have time to record anything. I peddled all I could. I was worried that my batteries wouldn't last for sixty miles, but they did.

The third day, we went to Farmville and the fourth day, we went to Richmond and stayed in the Catholic Cathedral. That was great. They gave us supper and breakfast.

The next night we went to Gum Spring and stayed at a winery. I slept in the shop on my air mattress in my sleeping bag.

The scenery was always beautiful. I don't write about it because that is just the way it is. I look around and I think I see mountains. I asked Nelson, "What are those things?" "They are mountains." I was not going to ride in mountains, but here I am. Oh, well, I had noticed it was going up and down a lot. It really wasn't bad. The ELF can coast up to 30 miles per hour. I was always way ahead of the group. Uphill it wasn't really too bad either. I guess I'll make it.

After that, we went to Culpeper. Some slept in their tent. A few of us went to town and got a motel room. I was one of them.

Then, we went to Middleburg. On the way there, a very huge dog came out of a farmyard. Sam was ahead of me. The dog charged at me but didn't know where he could get ahold of me. He tried my back tire. Nelson was behind me. The dog bit him in the butt. He really got him. We got a couple miles down the road to a wooded area. We stopped and Nelson exposed his rear so we could see where the dog had bit him. Boy, that dog really got him. The bite ruined his bicycle pants, too. Later on, they took him to the doctor, then went back to the farmer. The farmer had insurance. I don't know if they got something other than having the doctor bill paid. That was our only tragedy.

Later on, I had a flat tire. I told the guys to leave me behind. They don't need to wait for me. I'll go on my own. They would not hear of it. Sam loaded his bike in his pickup. There was a little house right where my tire went flat. I talked to the lady and asked if I could leave my bike there for a little bit until we figured out what to do. She was very nice.

The others went on to Middleburg and Sam and I drove to the nearest town and found a U-HAUL. We rented a trailer and picked up the bike. The next town had a bike shop. They fixed the tire. With all the stuff around it, the back tire is not easy to fix. I think the dog bit into it enough to puncture it a little. Oh, well, such is life.

We unloaded the bike in Middleburg. Sam and I took the trailer back and we were back in business. I don't remember where we slept. I think it was in a school building. We just slept on our air mattresses. It was all okay.

Friday, May 20, 2016

That night, we stopped at a very, very big farm. The farm was in the process of being sold. I didn't quite understand it. Some neighbors came by and they really celebrated the sale. I went to the second house on the property. It was being remodeled. I inflated my air mattress and went to sleep. In the night, it started pouring rain. Some slept in their tents and I was glad I didn't do that.

Washington D.C.

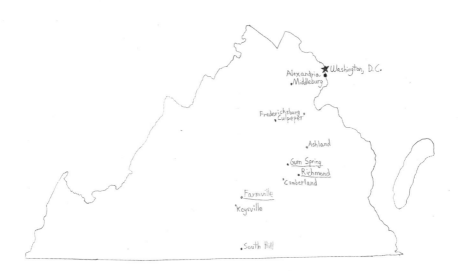

Saturday, May 21, 2016

In the morning, we had breakfast and decided to have the bikes hauled to Washington DC. It was easy to haul the regular bikes, but my monster was another story. One of the guys had a big flatbed on his pickup. He was hauling a lot of stuff for the group. We shuffled everything around so that we could load my ELF onto the flatbed. It had stopped raining by the time we got to Washington. George, a friend of Sam's, came to meet us. He doesn't live far from the Washington Memorial, where he met us. He had a bunch of flags for us to carry as we ride over the bridge to the Lincoln Memorial.

To be honest with you, I didn't know what was going on most of the time. I just went along. Across the road from the Lincoln Memorial was

Roger built the replica of the Bell Tower from the State University in Raleigh, North Carolina. People can take one of the outer panels, write something on it, and then replace it.

a huge park. Sam had sent Roger to Washington a few days ahead of us. Roger had built a replica of the bell tower. That was set up in the park. Also, a huge tent from the Vietnam Era was set up for us. Very impressive.

I was escorted to George's house. It was only three or four miles from the park. The houses are old and long, tall brick buildings with little tiny front yards. My bike didn't fit in George's front yard. We put it across the street in the neighbor's front yard. I had no way to lock the bike up. Originally, I had brought all kinds of stuff with me so I could lock the bike up; a heavy chain, a lock, a whole bunch of tools, and I don't know what all. I left those things somewhere along my journey when the bike broke down and I thought those heavy things were the cause. I decided no one would steal that bike, but George didn't trust the situation. He got a chain and locked that baby up.

We stayed the first night at George's. We slept on couches and air mattresses. The men slept upstairs.

Sunday, May 22, 2016

Most of those who had stayed overnight went home, including Sam. It was Sam's 91st Birthday today.

Someone escorted me back to the Lincoln Memorial Park. First, I had to get my bike freed and out of that yard. Then, we went back to where the tower was. I found out that the tower and the tent had to be watched 24 hours. I said I could stay there. They had cots, food and all kinds of stuff in the tent. I would be happy there. At night, they had someone come and stay with me in the tent.

I still didn't know what was going on, I never did really figure the whole thing out. I was in Washington and I saw a lot of things. I was happy as a clam. During the day, Roger was with the tower most of the time. I left my ELF sit there and walked around Washington by myself.

Friday, May 27, 2016

I was just standing around outside of the tent when I heard my name. I saw an Asian couple. The woman had been following me on Facebook and now she found me here. I was so happy and excited, I forgot to get her name or take her picture. I never thought in my wildest dreams that I would be writing a book. At the same time a guy came along who, also, had followed me on Facebook. He has an ELF. He saw my ELF. It was across the street from the tent next to a building where I could plug it in to charge the batteries. He started looking for me and found me. We went to look at my bike. There were several Veterans from the ROLLING THUNDER, a really big motorcycle group, looking over the ELF. It was all too exciting.

In the evening, I met Lorie, a wife of a Vietnam fallen soldier. I am so glad I decided to stay, even with thousands of motorcycles showing up the next day.

As I am writing all this stuff my emotions get the best of me. At least no one can see me. It is four in the morning. I wonder how many people write at night.

Tuesday, May 31, 2016

They took the tower down. The tent and everything was packed up and everyone left, except for me. I originally had planned to go to New York, but I decided against that. I thought I would take the easy way and go back to where I already know people. I know people like Jack and Georgia Tayler that helped me get across Georgia. They showed me the little bitty town of Calvary, where the Lions host Mule Day the first week in November. I told Jack that I would be back for that. I hadn't forgotten that.

Virginia 2

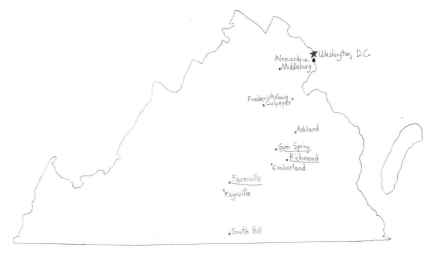

The roads I traveled in Virginia

Tuesday, May 31, 2016

I headed to Alexandria, VA. It wasn't easy to get out of Washington. They showed me a bike trail, but it always had barricades, which weren't always easy to get around. I finally made it to Alexandria. What a beautiful city. I went into a supermarket in the middle of the city. It was beautiful, and I always talked to beautiful people.

My one tire was low on air. I went past a bike shop. They checked all of the tires. They pumped them up for me. There are always good and helpful people wherever I go or have been. People asked me, "Aren't you afraid?" "No," I answered, "I'm still looking for the bad guy!"

Wednesday, June 1, 2016

Good Morning, America! I am totally alone. I don't know anyone. I am okay. It is six in the morning. I went to the office of the motel. They had a coffee pot going and I had some snack bars. I sat down at the table and visited with the boss.

About 8 am, a lady came through a door that looked like only the boss would have come through. I was wrong. There was a motel room behind that door. We got to visiting. I told her which vehicle in the parking lot was mine. She was very interested. We went out and looked at it. I think she was about my age, but very agile. I told her to crawl in and ride it. She was about my height, so I didn't have to adjust the seat. She rode around in the parking lot and had a really good time. She lived in Southern Pines, North Carolina. She invited me to stay at her house when I get to NC. I got her phone number and address. She left that morning and so did I.

I fumbled my way through the town. After a lot of riding, I realized I had never left Alexandria. It was evening. I had ridden all day and never left town. I saw a motel, went in and got a room. I will leave Alexandria tomorrow.

Thursday, June 2, 2016

I started out ready to make tracks. I set my GPS for some town, but I had to make some copies of the papers that I handed out. I usually had them make 100 copies for me at a print shop. I saw a shopping center. I went in there and looked around. I was not in any hurry to go anywhere. I talked to people. That was never a problem because of the ELF. I found a print shop and had my copies made.

I was almost afternoon. I thought I better get going. My GPS kept telling me to turn around. It said to make a U-turn. Over and over. I it said that. Finally, I got tired of listening to it. I shut it off. I rode maybe five, six or seven miles. I was on a four-lane highway with a nice shoulder. It was easy riding.

Finally, I pulled off the road and looked at the map to see if I really was going the wrong way. I was going north, and I wanted to go south. I turned around and went back. I was kind of frustrated, to say the least. I stopped at a supermarket to cool my jets a little bit. I must have been outside Alexandria somewhere. I really didn't know where I was at all.

I went in a grocery store. I saw a pair of twins about two years old. One had crawled out of the baby stroller shopping cart. They were having a great time. The mother had seen me outside with the ELF tricycle; now she asked me if I was the one riding it. "Yes." I said with a smile. Of course, we got in conversation. When we finished, she gave me her phone number and address. Her name was Emily. "If you want to, you can stay at our house tonight." "Well," I said, "I haven't gotten very far today. I don't know what I am going to do yet." She left and I wandered around aimlessly in the grocery store. I went to the parking lot. I looked at the map. It was about 3 pm. I gave Emily a call and said that I had decided to stay at her house. She sounded very happy. She gave me good directions on how to get to her house. As I was riding, I went past the motel that I stayed in the night before.

When I got to her house, she had to pick up her son from Kindergarten. We walked there. It was fun.

I made friends with the twins right away. Their names were Desmond and Victor. Travis was five. He was adopted. I don't remember from which Asian country. They were all nice boys. Emily's husband was in the Military in Iraq.

I stayed at their house four nights. I would have liked to just stay there and help her with the twins, but I had to keep going. It was like being with Caleb and Greta many years ago.

Sunday, June 5, 2016

Emily showed me how to get on the highway and going in the right direction. It was all meant to be the way it happened. I was to be with Emily for just a few days. (Much later I will meet Emily again.)

Monday, June 6, 2016

I am not clear about where I went, but I wrote on my Facebook page that I stayed in Dumfries at the Super 8 Motel.

Tuesday, June 7, 2016

I rode to Fredericksburg and stayed with Lion Wilma. The next evening, we went to a Lions Charter meeting.

Friday, June 10, 2016

I left early to go to Ashland, Virginia. I wasn't feeling the best. I thought
to myself, 'the first motel I see, I will spend the night there.' It was about
4 pm when I arrived at the edge of town and there, on the right-hand
side, was a motel. I got signed in. He was going to give me a room way
on the other end. When I said I needed a plug-in for my bike, he gave
me room number seventeen. I didn't feel good, so I went right to bed.
The chain that is usually on the door was ripped off. I could see daylight
through the side of the door. I wasn't worried. When I plugged in my
bike, some people were interested in the bike. I talked to them. They all
seemed very nice.

I was sound asleep. At about 10 pm, a fight broke out right in the room
next to me. Then, they went outside of my room. One of guys fell down
not far from my door. If he hit my door, he would fall right into my
room. I wasn't afraid, but thought I better call 911 for the first time in
my life. I called that number. The lady that answered the phone wasn't
too terribly nice. I didn't remember the name of the motel. I didn't want
to turn the light on, because I didn't want them to know that I called.
Then she heard them yelling. "Is that those guys?" I said, "Yes." I think
she thought I was part of the fight. When she realized that I wasn't, she
changed her tune and was very nice.

The next day it was in the paper that the guy next door to me had beaten
up two other guys by using a machete. If I would have gotten the room
that the owner of the motel was going to give me at first, way on the other end, I would have not called 911. One of the guys could have bled to
death if I had not called. They had two police cars and two ambulances
there. They were there for a very long time.

It could have been scary, but I was never nervous. That is unusual for
me. Again, I was meant to be there.

I left the motel in the morning and went to Hardees and had breakfast. I never said anything to anybody about what happened the night before. I didn't write it on my Facebook page, but I thought I would share the story in my book.

Saturday, June 11, 2016

I needed to do laundry. Just little way along the main road I saw a laundromat. I had no sooner stopped my bike, when an older man came out of the laundromat to talk to me. He owned the business. He loved my bike. He said he was an electrician and he liked the solar panel. It didn't look like I was going to get any laundry done. That was okay. He wanted to introduce me to some people in town. One of the ladies I met said they should get the newspaper and have me interviewed. Another woman, who had come from the coffee shop said, "She is sitting right in the coffee shop." I went in there and that's how I met Natalie Miller. She interviewed me for their paper. She, also, invited me to her house. I didn't have time that day because I was supposed to meet Lion District Governor Lee Winder in Richmond that afternoon. It was already 11 am and I had quite a way to go.

It was 3 pm when I passed the State Police Station in Richmond. I went inside. I asked them if it would be possible to park my bike in their yard overnight. Their answer was, "Certainly." I called District Governor Lee and his wife, Lion Jane, and asked if they could pick me up at the police station. They were going to take me to a Lions meeting. It all worked out perfectly. I stayed overnight at Winder's house in Richmond. In the morning, they took me back to my bike.

Sunday, June 12, 2016

I rode back to Ashland, VA. I got a motel room and called Natalie. She invited me to come to her parents' house the next day. I am still not feeling totally well. I went to bed early, so, hopefully, I would feel better in the morning.

Monday, June 20, 2016

I met Natalie and her mother, Angela, at a restaurant downtown. We ate something and they escorted me to their house. They live a little bit out of the town in a new housing development. I stayed at Miller's house until the 23rd of June. I peddled around town every day. It is a very nice town. The railroad goes right through the middle of town. The railroad tracks have special crossings that get you from one side of the street to the shops on the other side of the street. It is a beautiful, picturesque city.

I spent most days pedaling around town and visiting with people and with Angela, when she had time. She told me about her husband, Torens' dad that was 90 some years old and in good shape. He had been in WWll on the front line. I love to talk to those people. He lived in Massillon, Ohio. I looked at my Atlas and I thought about renting a car a nd driving to Ohio. I told Angie that. She said, "I'll drive you there. We go there lots of times. It takes eight hours to get there. We can have supper with him and visit with him. We can stay overnight with Torens' sister and come home." That's what we did. Whenever I talk to a WWll veteran, I get terribly emotional. Thank God Angie was with me. She is a very strong person and keeps me laughing all the time.

She doesn't like deer, because they eat all her flowers. I don't know which flowers she likes but the deer like them a lot, too. She has a back yard full of flowers and her front yard is, too. They have tried all kinds of stuff to stop the deer. Nothing they have tried works. When she was driving to Massillon, Ohio and she saw a dead deer on the side of the road she reached her arm across the front of me and she would go, "Bang, bang, bang." I would say, "It is dead already." She would say, "But I have to make sure". We did a lot of laughing.

It was absolutely great to meet Torens' father. We visited and visited about the war and all kinds of stuff. He was still in good shape. His wife had died, I think, a couple years ago. I thanked him for coming to Germany because, if the Americans wouldn't have come, I would not be here. That story is hard for me to tell. But I have to tell it and thank the American people, especially the WW ll soldiers. There are not many of them left. I kind of let him lead the conversations because a lot of people that have been in the thick of war don't like to talk about it that much and he had been in the thick of it.

Tuesday, June 21, 2016

We had a wonderful stay at Torens' sister and brother-in-law's house. We took Torens' Dad out for breakfast. We said our goodbyes and went home. At 5 pm we were back at Angie's house in Ashland.

Wednesday, June 22, 2016

I was feeling very bad. I had been there two weeks. Angie would not let me leave until we went to the doctor. She took me to a walk-in clinic. They took a chest x-ray. I had bronchitis. They prescribed antibiotics. Thank goodness, I had U-Care Supplemental Insurance. That practically paid for everything. I recovered quickly.

Friday, June 24, 2016

I was well now. I had to finish taking my antibiotics, but I felt great. I hadn't felt that good for quite some time.

I left that morning for Gum Springs to the winery where we stayed when I was traveling with the Veterans for Peace. We didn't visit much when I was traveling with the group. I did meet an older retired couple who had asked me to come back when I was in the area again. So, I did. They seemed to be delighted. The winery was called the Gray Haven Winery. The older couple escorted me to a camp- ground about 40 miles away from where they lived. I stayed overnight at the campground.

Saturday, June 25, 2016

It was a very nice campground and nice people were in the office. They were all interested in the ELF, like always. I had started putting my tent up when a guy on a 4-wheeler stopped by and asked if he could help me. I accepted the help. He told me that he and his wife stay there free for about six months as helpers. Then they go to another campground. All they need to do is check the fire pits and a few other things and help the campers with any problems they have. I don't remember what they call them; I think that they're kind of a host camper or something like that. It is a nice idea. I sure appreciated the help. He, also, invited me to their RV for supper. It was great. We visited long into the evening.

I don't remember much about the next few days. I have notes and names, but nothing shakes my memory.

Sunday, June 26, 2016

I wrote on my calendar that I am in Cumberland and went to church with Lynn and Chuck. I have no recollection of them. If you are reading this, I am very sorry.

Let me tell you about Sandy:

I am riding through Farmville. Farmville is a big city with all kinds of highways going all kinds of directions. I pull into Mc Donald's to get some ice cream and figure out which way to go to get to Keysville. A lady standing next to me in line said, "I saw you stopped along the highway. I was wondering if you were okay?" That was Sandi. I got my ice cream and joined her at her table. Sandi lives in Farmville but has a business in Keysville. We exchanged stories about our lives, and I told her that I belong to the Lions and so on. She told me which highway to take to get to Keysville and that there is only one hotel. It is a family-owned hotel called Sheldon, after the family name. It is about 20 miles from here. It was 3 pm. I was in good shape.

When I was about five miles away from Keysville, my phone rings. It is Sandi. She tells me that there was a room reserved for me at Sheldon's. When I got there, Sandi stood there with a Keysville Lion.

I was so happy to be able to greet a Lion.

So, there we have it again, the great, caring, generous people of the United States, always helping a total stranger.

I can't remember what all happened in the next three days. I have names written down but nothing else.

I am on good roads and daydream.

Concentration Camps

During WWll, they built concentration camps all over Germany and other countries. There was one built 25 miles from my parents' house. I learned about it 20 years ago. When my mother was still alive, I went to Germany every year for her birthday in January. I was driving with a friend, Armin Guckenholz, to his house when we passed Bergen-Belsen Concentration Camp. I said, "Can we go in there?" He said, "Let's go there." We did. (You can look it up on the internet. It can make you sick, but I am glad I went. I had no idea it was that close to us. My parents didn't know that either. They were told it was for prisoners of war.) We looked around. They had some heart-wrenching pictures of the place. That's where Anne Frank died. We left after seeing enough. A person cannot comprehend something like that happening.

There was a farm not far from there that had a sign saying, "Coffee House." We stopped there for coffee. An older man greeted us. We told him that we had just been at the museum. This was what he said: "THOSE LIES! I DON'T KNOW HOW THEY GET BY WITH THOSE LIES!!!!!!!"

It was like somebody poured cold water over us. How is it, that there are still people thinking it never happened?

We had our coffee and left. No one said anything. There just wasn't anything to say.

THANK GOD THE AMERICANS CAME! I SAID IT BEFORE, BUT I AM GOING TO SAY IT AGAIN!

IF YOU WOULD NOT HAVE COME WHEN YOU DID, I WOULN'T BE WRITING THIS BOOK.

THANK YOU AGAIN AND AGAIN !!!! MY USA, MY HOME!!!!!!!

Armin Guckenholz

Now I will tell you how I met Armin Guckenholz from Germany. In 1986, my daughter, Andrea, spent a year in Germany with my mother and my brother, Manfred. She met a lot of people over there. A few years later, a girl named Frauke wrote me a letter saying she didn't know anybody in the USA. She would like to come and wanted to know if she could come to our house. I wrote her a letter saying that, in a month, I would be in Germany and I could come to see her and we could talk about it.

My brother, Manfred, drove me to her house, which was in a small town about 25 miles from my mother's house. When we got there, a young man was sitting next to Frauke. His name was Jochen. I asked him if he had been to the USA. His answer was no, but he would like to come sometime. I told him he should come with Frauke. That's what happened. They came almost at the same time as I got back from Germany.

We had a good time. Frauke had to go back after one month. Jochen stayed a half of year. He lived on a farm in Germany and the farmers have to go through an apprenticeship like all the other trades people. His dad had an apprentice while Jochen was with me.

When Jochen got back to Germany, his father's school friend was visiting. His name was Armin Guckenholz. He was talking about going to the USA. Jochen asked where in the USA he was going. "Ach," Armin said, "You wouldn't know where I am going. It is a long way into the country, La Crosse, Wisconsin." "I know where that is. It isn't far from where I have been. When you get there, you give Hanna a call. She would like that."

It was in the fall. We were in the middle of filling the silo. The phone rings in the barn. I answered it. It was Armin. I invited him for coffee and cake the next day in the afternoon.

Armin is a very social guy. He tells me that he has a school friend in La Crosse that he has been visiting. He comes to the USA every other year. He stays for three months. In Germany, he lays TV cable. He has a pretty

big company. He has a manager, but his wife helps with some of the money-handling.

As he left, he invited me to his house when I come to Germany. I was there in January for my mother's birthday. Armin picked me up in Verden and drove me to his house in Hannover, about an hour from Verden. I met his wife and she went with us to Jochen's farm. Over the years, we all became good friends.

That's how Armin Guckenholz came into our lives. Armin passed away two years ago. Armin made sure that his daughter and son-in-law took over the tradition of visiting the USA. Udo and Maria were here in the summer of 2019.

Monday, June 27, 2016

I am in Keysville.

Tuesday, June 28, 2016

I am in South Boston in a motel with new owners.

June 29 and June 30, 2016

My memory is not serving me well.

Friday, July 1, 2016

I was asked by Sam, the leader of the Veterans for Peace group, to stop by his place in Leasburg, North Carolina. I will go there now.

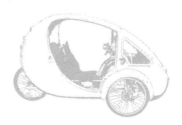

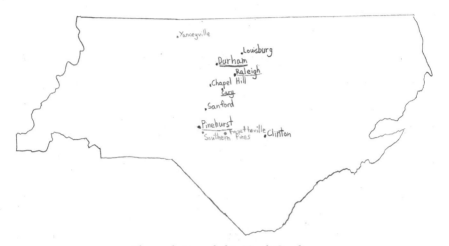

The roads I traveled in North Carolina

Friday, July 1, 2016

I stopped at Sam's. He lives in Leasburg with his wife. I had a good time. I met his sister that lived a few miles from Sam. Across the road lived another relative that I met who later escorted me to town, where I had a flat tire. He helped me to get some gobbledegook to put in the tire. That worked well until I got to Organic Transport in Durham, North Carolina.

Thursday, July 7, 2016

I went back to Organic Transit in Durham. I slept in the office again. They did some more repairs to my bike. They replaced some Duct tape, among other things. There was enough time to ride to Wendy's house in Cary. I called her and everything is always okay with her. I took off, but about half-way to her house, the bike stopped. It was dead; really dead.

I called Organic Transit. It was about 4 pm and they hadn't left yet. They came with their big van and picked up the ELF. I called Wendy and she met me. You know those fancy I-phones we would sometimes like to throw in the ditch? In a case like this, they come in mighty handy. I gave her the street I was on and she found me with no problem. What luck that the ELF's motor broke down around Durham.

Saturday, July 9, 2016

Mike delivered the ELF back to me. Mike and his family live close to Wendy's. I invited Mike and his family and Wendy's family to a German restaurant for a meal. I felt I owed them all something. It was very nice.

Monday, July 11, 2016

I tried to ride the ELF to Raleigh. Well, with my sense of direction, it's hopeless. I think I am directionally dyslexic, but I got there somehow or other. Suddenly, I was at the University. It was already noon. It took me all morning to go ten miles. I parked my bike in sort of a park at the University. I walked across the road to a shop where they make signs. I wanted one of Raleigh. Next, in comes the guy from Iran that was with his wife and two small children on our trip to Washington D.C. He saw my bike and found me in the store. It was such a wonderful surprise. He took me to the University to his wife's class that she was teaching. What an exciting meeting for all of us. How can that happen?

On the way back to Wendy's house, I actually went the right way. It was easy and a relatively short stretch.

Tuesday, July 12, 2016

I called Roy and Billy Jernigan and asked if I could come back to their house. They were, also, delighted to have me come back. It was kind of nice to see people again.

Wednesday, July 13, 2016

Now I went back to Pinehurst to Jan and Ron. I stayed there four nights. We went to a few Lions meetings. I love going to meetings. I really do.

The Lions are always very positive, and they always want to help. Well, that's what we do; We Serve.

Sunday, July 17, 2016

Remember the lady I met in Virginia that invited me to her house when I got to North Carolina? She lived only eight miles from Jan and Ron in Southern Pines. I shouldn't have too much trouble finding them and I didn't. When I got to her house, she had just gone to the store. I met her husband, Mike. Just a few minutes later, Sue came home. What a great reunion.

Sue is a small wiry lady. She is very agile. I know now why; she taught gymnastics all her life. I don't remember for sure, but I think she is older than I am or the same age. She runs every day down her street and back up. I jogged along. She went kiddy corner back and forth like a rabbit. I could not keep up with her.

Wednesday, July 20, 2016

I had told Jan, my previous host, about the book I got from a young nurses' aide at Madonna Towers when my mother died about ten or fifteen years ago. It is a children's book. I like it so much that, whenever I go to a funeral, I buy that book in place of a sympathy card. I was going to buy one for Jan, but I didn't find it anywhere in Southern Pines. Sue drove me to Fayetteville to Barnes and Noble. They had one book left. It is called: 'THE NEXT PLACE' by Warren Hanson; I mailed that book to Jan Kelly.

When we got back, Mike came to me and said, "I hope you don't mind, but I got ahold of a Toastmaster and we can go to a meeting tonight at the college." I could have hugged him; it made me that happy.

You see, when I started my trip, besides the Lions, I was going to promote Toastmasters. Some people knew about Lions, but hardly anybody knew about Toastmasters. I gave up on promoting Toastmasters.

I had told this story in conversation to Mike and Sue. While we were gone, Mike took it upon himself and researched Toastmasters.

We went to the meeting that evening. Mike and Sue enjoyed it, and I definitely liked it a lot. Not only that, but the president invited me to his house to have my picture taken in his backyard and sent to Toastmasters International to go in their magazine on traveling Toastmasters. The next day, Mike escorted me to the president's house. They had a pond in the backyard. It was just beautiful. I could see why he wanted us to come there.

WHAT FUN!!!!!!!!!!!!

Another thing that happen in Southern Pines: I was riding around when I spotted a little shop with purses and other things made from materials left over from the military made by military wives. I went in the store and was greeted by three young women. They saw me on the sidewalk riding the ELF. I asked them if they would like to ride it? Of course, they would. They rode it, one after the other. It was fun seeing them having fun.

I bought a purse. I don't normally have a purse, especially on this journey. But, in order to support this great company, I bought one. I wrote a check for $150.00. They took it, but never cashed it. I didn't know it until I got home.

THANK YOU, R. RIVERTER!!!!!!!!! I will keep that purse forever. It fit right in my backpack. When I went somewhere special on my journey, I just pulled it out of my backpack. It worked out beautifully.

Saturday, July 23, 2016

On my way to Rockingham, I stayed in a motel. To be honest with you, again, my memory is failing me. I am sure it was an event for the people, like always. It repeats itself, time and time again.

South Carolina 2

The roads I traveled in South Carolina

Sunday, July 24, 2016

I'm on my way to Cheraw, South Carolina. I was there before. Sue Redman lives in the woods. My GPS misled me last time. This time, I came from the other end of town. I was feeling a little woozy. It is July. It is very hot, like 100 degrees. I had a lot of water with me. I poured some over my head. That water was warm. It didn't help much. I saw very few houses and they were a few miles apart. I asked myself, 'Should I stop at this house? I better, I can't even think straight.' I drove into their driveway. A lady came to the door. "Can I help you?" I said, "I think I am in trouble with the heat." She welcomed me into the house and got wet wash cloths for me. I started to tell her and her husband what I was doing and where I was heading. After a while, I asked them if I could call Susan Redman. "I met her the other day at a funeral," the lady said. I called Susan and told her what had happened and that I can leave my bike here. The lady of the house talked to Susan. After she hung up, she said " I'll take you to her house. It is only four miles from here."

There are so many people to thank all the time. I still haven't found the bad guy.

Monday, July 25, 2016

In the morning, we picked up my bike. Then, I had to figure out what to do. I could stop my journey, or I can try starting first thing in the morning and riding until noon. I'll see how that works. If that doesn't work, I will have to quit.

I stayed four days at Susan's until I had totally recovered.

Friday, July 29, 2016

I am riding my ELF to McBee. It is nice to know people I can call, like Angela. I couldn't stay at their house because Leon, her husband, was going to have open heart surgery on Monday, but she would find somebody. She did. John Martin has a shipping container that he made into a house. He has a factory where he spends Monday through Thursday and then he goes back to his real home along the beach. The shipping container is unoccupied for three days. That's where I made myself at home for two nights. It was fun and very nice. When I was inside, I had no idea that I was in a shipping container.

Monday, August 1, 2016

Now I am riding back to Richard Pinkerton and family in Camden, South Carolina. I am riding right along. It is amazing that I can go about 40 miles or so in a day.

Tuesday, August 2, 2016

I am in Stateburg, South Carolina. There was one not-so-good motel. I had no choice. I had been riding over 50 Miles with nothing in-between and who knows were the next motel will be. The people were very nice to me. Later in the evening, a guy came by that was an engineer from Belgium. He was here for a month or two. A few miles down the road was a big factory where he worked. They gave me a room two doors down from his.

It was a little town. I scoped it out a little bit. They had a very small restaurant/grocery store. It was enough for me to get by. There were a few houses and a community center or something like that.

At two in the morning, someone knocked on my door. To be honest, I was a little bit scared. I ignored it. A little bit later, a car drove away. I was very happy.

Wednesday, August 3, 2016

I stopped in St. Mathews. I am not sure what it is about this town, but I feel very emotional as I am peddling into town. I left the motel at Stateburg at 6:15 am. I rode two hours and never stopped. I don't think I have ever done that, however, there really never was a place to stop. I stopped at the first available place and that was Hardee's in St. Mathews.

I came through this town in March. At that time, I stopped at an older gas station. Actually, I rode past the station. I had stopped to figure out where I had to go. The station attendant, the owner, Richard Thornton, caught up with me. He wanted to know about that thing I was riding. We visited as I pushed my bike to the station. He invited me in. I saw books on a shelf. I was paging through one, with the plan to buy it. Richard informed me that he wrote that book. He signed it for me and said, "That is my present for you." We visited a little more and I went on my way.

That's probably why I felt so sentimental about that town.

Now, I am at Hardees. It is 8:15 am. What chance will I have to see that guy that wrote the book sometime during the day? I ordered something and sat down. A big table was occupied by elderly people dressed for church. I observed the group. After a bit, they all got up and left. When the last couple started to walk out, I gathered enough courage to walk up to them because the guy had about the same build as I remembered

Richard Thornton having. The wife reminded me of Clarabelle Voelker, my sponsors in Iowa 50 years ago. I asked the guy if he had written a book? Can you believe it? That was the man, RICHARD HAMPTON THORNTON SR. They were on their way to a funeral, so there was not much time to visit.

Thursday, August 4 through Sunday, August 7, 2016

All I remember is that I was in Orangeburg, Bamberg, Hampton, SC

16
Hanna's
Dream
Ride

Georgia 2

The roads I traveled in Georgia

Monday August 8, 2016

I am back in Sylvania, Georgia. I stayed at the Sylvania Inn. I just want to make a comment about staying in motels and any other commercial place where I stayed: it was great in every place. I never experienced any bad treatment in any way, shape or form. As I always say, *"It is because of the ELF."*

Tuesday, August 9, 2016

It's only 24 miles to Statesboro, Georgia. Because of the heat, I only go a short stretch. I stayed at the Red Roof Inn.

Wednesday, August 10, 2016

I arrived in Claxton at 9 am. I went to McDonald's until I could check in to a motel.

Thursday, August 11, 2016

I called ahead to Lyon, Georgia. Lion Larry and Debbie Griggers were out of town. They told me they could unlock the doors with their phone. They have a dog sitter come in two times a day. I said I'd rather get there when the dog sitter is there. And that's what I did. I arrived at 9:30 am. The dog sitter was there and let me in. I visited with her for a couple of hours. She explained the security system. Well, it is needless to say, I had trouble with it. But, not to worry, they could tell from their phone when I was in trouble. They always fixed it for me. I left at the same time the dog sitter left. In the evening, I came back when the dog sitter came back. Everything was okay. The dog sitter locked everything up when she left. The next morning, she came back. We did the same thing every day. I left at the same time she left. I just looked around town and a neighboring town. I had a great time.

Saturday, August 13, 2016

This day, I rode my bike to Vidalia. That's where the Vidalia onions come from. I guess there's a special kind of soil that makes those onions very sweet. It was a very interesting town.

Sunday, August 14, 2016

Debbie and Larry are coming home. What joy. Larry told me the last time that I was there, that he had started writing a book. I read it and it was great. I said that he should set a date for when he plans on having it done. Someday will never come. I told him stories about myself and how I had planned this journey since I was in my twenties. I was going to Texas on my bike. That was all I had at the time. I was going kind of like a hobo. I would work my way to Texas. If it took two years, it didn't matter. When I told my sponsors about my plans, they said, "Hanna, that is too dangerous." I got to go to Texas, but not on my bike.

I never gave up on that dream. One has to be footloose and fancy-free to do something that crazy. Life took me in all kinds of directions. I thought to myself, 'When I am 80 years old, if I live that long, I will be footloose and fancy-free.' Well, I did it sooner, but if I had given up on that dream and not set a date, I would have forgotten about it.

Debbie had nicely printed "SET A DATE, SOMEDAY NEVER COMES!" and put it in a frame and put it where everyone could see it. That was quite the honor to see that. Thanks, Debbie.

Tuesday, August 16, 2016

Larry and Debbie insisted on trailering my bike to McRae to a motel where I spent the night. Again, super nice help. I am still looking for the bad guy.

Someone met me. (I am sorry I didn't keep a very good record at that time.) I can't, for the life of me, remember who trailered my bike to the Georgia Veteran's Memorial State Park Hotel in Cordele, Georgia. I thought I was dreaming. That was one of the most beautiful hotels I have been in.

Boy, I wish I knew who took me there. She was a police person. Maybe I will find out before this book gets printed.

There was a huge park around the hotel. I was just walking around, when, suddenly, my phone rang.

It was Emily from Virginia! Can you believe that? She is the lady with the twins. She saw my bike. She was staying with her parents and her in-laws less than a mile away. It was unbelievable. I can't describe how happy both of us were. I stayed at the very fancy hotel for one night.

Thursday, August 18, 2016 - Sunday, August 21, 2016

I stayed with Emily's in-laws because they had a big house.

Monday, August 22, 2016

Emily had to go pick up her husband in Atlanta. He was on leave from Iraq. I left that morning and rode through Plains, which I looked at a little bit. I ended up in Americus, where I stayed with Lewis and Mary Overholt again.

Alice and her husband in their yard

Tuesday, August 23, 2016

I went to Seale, where I stayed with Alice.

Wednesday, August 24, 2016 – Sunday, August 28, 2016

I continued to stay with Alice.

Monday, August 29, 2016

I left my bike at Alice's. (She made my meeting with Jimmy Carter possible.) Alice took me to Columbus, Georgia to the airport to go to Rochester, Minnesota.

I had registered to go to the US-Canada Forum in Omaha, Nebraska on September 15.

It was great to be in Minnesota. My grandchildren welcomed me home, like always. They are at the growing age. They have changed in the time I have been gone. Armin was 14 years old. His voice had changed, and he was getting taller. Silvia is 13 years old. They both have grown a lot. They always have made a nice card for me.

Tuesday, August 30, 2016 – Wednesday, September 14, 2016

I stayed in Minnesota.

Thursday, September 15, 2016

My friend, Jan, drove her vehicle all the way to Omaha, Nebraska. We made it one day. I made sandwiches and refreshments. It was great. It is always an organized commotion at those forums. I like it. The Lions are always in a good mood. I see people that I have met before.

What can I say about the US-Canada educational forum? It is great. You just have to make a plan to go to one of them yourself to understand why I get excited about something like that.

I find it very inspiring when we sing each other's national anthem.

 US Canada Forum Etcetera

I remember the first US-CANADA Forum I went to. It was in Peoria, Illinois. We went on a bus. It was in 2005. Brian Sheehan, who will be the Lions International President in 2021, was council chair that year. He organized the bus ride. He entertained all of us and he has the best, infectious laugh. Always in a good mood. He lives in Bird Island, Minnesota, a town of 1000 people. In 2021, it will be exactly 100 years since Minnesota had an International President in the Lions organization.

We are all very proud of you, Brian!!!!!!!!!

Years back, in 1997, Willie Eppen invited me to a Lions meeting. I joined the Lions. It wasn't long after that they had an International Convention in Indianapolis, Indiana. I asked Willie if I could go to that? He said, "Sure you can." He wasn't going that year. I didn't know any Lions outside of the Chatfield club. I mean, I didn't know one single soul. Willie had been District Governor, so he knew all about Lions. He knew a lot of people outside of our club. I went, by myself, that's when I got the Lion fever. Since then I go to everything that I can go to.

I didn't even know the different lingo that was used, like a Plenary session. I thought that they sit around and make plans. Was I wrong!

They had buses to haul people from the hotel to the coliseum where all the events took place. I wandered around among the thousands of people from almost 200 countries. Now there are over 200 countries that have Lions clubs. It was a few years later, when I realized that the word Plenary had nothing to do with planning.

Lions serve. It's that simple, and it has been since we began in 1917. Our clubs are places where individuals join together to give their time and talents and resources to serve in their community and in the world. It is non-political and it doesn't matter what religion one belongs to.

It was in Japan at the International Convention, (Can you believe I went there? Well, I did.) that Roy Larson from Pine Island, MN was sworn in as District Governor of the District I was in. I saw Roy Larson in Japan at the very end of the convention. I didn't know that they had a special section for 5M1, my District, Lions with a snowman in the aisle. There are so many people and those places are so huge.

What I clearly remember is that I was at odds with my brothers in Germany to the point that I was not going to Germany again until my mother died. I was sitting in a huge coliseum at the convention. They were having the 'Parade of Flags'. Every country that has a Lions club was represented. It is so impressive. It is a tearjerker for me. The whole first floor was filled with Japanese Lions. I think there must have been thousands of them. I was told that the Japanese actually appreciated what the Americans did in WWll. We all know what happened in WWll. The Japanese had forgiven us, but I couldn't forgive my brothers for whatever I was mad at them

about. Am I nuts, or what? What is wrong with me? Now, I compared the price it cost for me to fly to Japan versus going to a shrink, a psychiatrist or psychologist, in order to forgive my brothers. The trip was a lot less expensive, a lot more fun, and more effective than a Doctor could have been. I forgave my brothers for whatever it was I was mad about and went back to Germany.

 ## US Canada Forum Etcetera

This story happened four days before the war ended in Germany. Two Nazi officers showed up at our farm. They talked to my dad. They wanted him to take the horse and ammunition to the French border. My father said something he should have never said. "We are going to lose the war." Normally, those officers would have shot him right then and there. But for some reason they didn't. They told him he had to harness up the horse. He said that his neighbor borrowed the harness. The officers told him to go to the neighbor and get the harness. My father left and went in the hayloft to hide in the hay. The officers went looking for him. They asked my mother where he was. My father didn't tell anybody that he was hiding. My mother called and called him. He never answered. Then the officers asked our hired man (knecht) in German. He was a rather small built guy. They told him to go get the harness from the neighbor. The hired guy told them he wouldn't do it unless his boss told him to. Those officers beat him up so bad they finally took his head and hit it on the cobblestone that the farmyard was plastered with. The hired guy finally got the harness, hooked up the horses, and took off to take some ammunition to the French border. We have no idea where in the hell he was supposed to go. But he took off. The American soldiers came, and the war ended a few days later.

My dad thought he'd never see the hired man again. Several weeks later, the hired man came back with the two horses. I don't remember whatever happened to him.

Monday, October 3, 2016

I flew back to Columbus, Georgia. Hannah Flynn picked me up at the airport and took me to her house in Greenville. Alice trailered my bike to Hannah Flynn's. Hannah took me around to different places. Greenville was a nice little city. Hannah lived a few miles out of town. That was just fine. I liked to ride around and talk to people. .

My plan was to get to Calvary for Mule Day by the first Saturday in November. I had plenty of time to get there.

I can't remember what all we did, and all the places Hannah Flynn and I went.

I got to Calvary a week early. I thought I would see someone from the Lions club. No such luck. There is nothing in that town. There are a few houses and sort of a hardware store with a few groceries. That's all. It was getting late. I didn't know what to do. I saw a lady walking into the store. I asked her if she knew somewhere that I could set up my tent. She took me to her sister's house. I was glad because I didn't know what else to do. It was close to the Florida border and there was nowhere that I could stay.

We visited until it got dark. I went in my tent and went to sleep.

I waited a while in the morning. I didn't hear or see anybody. I packed up my stuff, left them a note and left to go to Quincy, Florida. I called the people that I had stayed with before. Debbie was so happy to see me, she jumped up and down when I rode in with my bike.

I put my bike in the shed and plugged it in to get it charged up. In the morning, I unplugged it and got it out of the shed. I pushed the power button. It would not do anything. The batteries were fully charged. We called Organic Transit. They had me take pictures of the motor. Ron helped me with all of that. I don't know, we didn't really get anything accomplished. This was Monday, November 1st.

On Thursday, November 3rd Ron trailered the sick ELF to Calvary to the Lions building. Now, there were people there that gave me permission to stay in the Lions building overnight. That was great. I got up at 4 am. I heard something outside the building. I went out to see what all the racket was. There were all kinds of trucks and people unloading stuff for the festival. I asked them if I could help.

Glenda was a person going like crazy unloading a big truck. Right behind the Lions building there were cooking and grilling facilities. Glenda gladly accepted my help. She had a very nice enclosed trailer where she has all the cookware and all of the other stuff that she needs for the event. I had no idea how large that event was going to be. I was told that it was big, but that big?

Glenda had, I think, 15 huge pots. Each one had five chickens in it. They were being cooked and then all the meat was taken off for chicken combo. After a while, a lot of women came to help.

Cathy, one of the ladies that worked at Glenda and her husband's business, visited with me. I told her that I was there on my tricycle, but it was very broken at the time. She took me home with her that evening to Climax, Georgia. That was great.

The place was filled with people. They had permanent buildings on the complex. I was told that the Lions were working in one of the buildings. I met the head honcho, Janette Sickle. I visited with her and asked her if there was an electrician around. I was in luck. There was one working on an outlet in that building. She introduced me to him. His name was Dan Farnsworth. I asked him if he was related to Philo Farnsworth, who was a genius with electricity. Guess what, he was related to him. I asked Dan if he could help me with my bike. I needed to take a picture of the guts of the motor. As soon as he got done with the outlet, we walked over to my bike. We called Organic Transit and we got the job done. They were going to send the part to Dan. Later on, Dan picked up my bike and took it to his farm and put it in a shed.

The celebration, what can I say about it. It was huge. They had a long parade. Lots of mules were in it. One couple from Byron, Minnesota was among them. They saw my ELF sitting outside of the Lions building. They have the big horses that they use with a covered wagon. Their names were John and Monica Davis. John belongs to the Rochester Morning Pride Lions Club. Monica didn't go in the parade because she was looking for me. She finally found me. I can't tell you how happy I was to see people from Rochester. That far into Georgia in that very, very little town, it was a huge surprise.

I stayed a week with Cathy and Doug Griffin in Climax, Georgia. What a beautiful house with a very huge indoor swimming pool. Very impressive.

I talked to Dan Farnsworth. He had gotten the part. He put the part on and plugged it in and it blew up. He didn't know what to do.

Saturday, November 14, 2016

Nothing was getting done. I didn't know what to do. I rented a car and drove home to Minnesota. I wanted to be home for the Mid-Winter convention in January anyway.

I conversed over the phone with Dan but we didn't accomplished anything. Dan told me that I would have to get the ELF back to Organic Transit in Durum, N.C. They would be the only ones that would know what is wrong with it. Otherwise, if I take it to a bike shop, they wouldn't know what to do with it. That was that!

Back in Minnesota, I took part in watching my Grandkids at their piano recitals. I watched Caleb and Greta in a musical. All kinds of stuff happens around Christmas time, but I was very anxious to be back on my journey.

February 10, 2017

I flew back to Columbus, Georgia. Alice picked me up at the airport. The next day, she took me to Michelle and Mike Miller's in Bainbridge, Georgia. It looks like I will stay here for a while.

Boy, oh, boy, things don't look good for me to get together with my ELF. But I just roll with the punches. Everyone is treating me very, very well. I just get hauled around by mostly Lions. Everyone seems to be glad to take me to conventions. I am always glad to go with them.

Michelle and Mike are both working from home. Michelle is a teacher. I am not sure what Mike does. On the side, they were remodeling a house. I tried to help a little with that. Millers were gone for one weekend. I was being picked up by Janette to be taken to a convention in Americus. I was Hannah Flynn's roommate. Hannah took me back to Michelle Miller's mother, Jane, who also lives in Bainbridge.

We had picked up five bags of pecans a few days ago. Jane and I hulled them in one day. If you understand all of that, then you are doing well. I am not sure I got it right.

Friday, February 24, 2017

I am back at Mike and Michelle Miller's. Hanna Flynn picked me up to take me to Savannah, Georgia to go to their State Lions Convention. I won't be coming back to the Miller's. Always the good-byes were hard, especially when I stayed so long in one place that I was shooting roots.

Hannah took good care of me at the convention. After the convention, she showed me the ship port. I was very impressed with that. It brought memories back from when I left Bremerhaven, Germany in 1961. Boy, oh, boy, did that bring back memories!

I went home with Hannah to Greenville. I can't tell you what all we did. All I can tell you is that Hannah is a very, very busy Lion. She is involved in so, so, many things. I always rode with her. She is older than I am, but she hops around like a young filly.

I stayed in touch with Dan Farnsworth. He kept telling me that I have to get the bike back to Organic Transit. Well, I tried different things like U-Haul and other options. It is a long way to Durham and it costs a lot of money.

Thursday, March 9, 2017

Hannah took me to her Lions meeting. We were there early and so was a gentleman, Bill Campbell. I overheard him saying that he was so tired. I asked him if he worked nights. "No." He said that he had driven a truck to Durham, North Carolina. I popped up and said, "North Carolina? That's too bad. That's where I need to take my ELF." He said, "I can get it there for you. That company I work for is very good. I'll see what I can do. Otherwise, I have a trailer. We'll get your bike to Durham."

H A L L E L U J A H !!!!!!!!!!!!!!!!!!!! I AM SPEECHLESS!!!!!!!!!!!!!!!!

Besides the Lions, Bill belongs to the Masons. He invited Hannah and me to his meeting on Sunday evening. I kept asking Bill if that wasn't asking too much for him to take me to Durham. "No," he said. "I got it figured out. I'll take my trailer and I'll take you. That is no problem. My children don't live that far from Durham. That gives me a chance to see them. We go practically right past them."

I gave a little talk that evening at the Masons meeting. I told them that in Seymour, Indiana I walked into a restaurant full of Masons. They connected me with a Lion. I stayed overnight with a Mason. All in all, they treated me like royalty. They really did. At the end of that meeting that evening, they were discussing who was paying for the gas in Bill's vehicle. I kind of overheard the conversation. I popped up and said, "I am going to pay for the gas, for sure." It was silent. I found out later on that the Masons gave Bill money for the gas. What can I say? Thank you! Thank you! To Bill and his wife, Fonda, to the Masons, to Hannah Flynn and so many, many more.

THANK YOU, AMERICA!!!!!!!!!!!!!!!!

As I am writing this, I am slobbering all over this keyboard. Sorry, I am getting emotional all over again.

Monday, March 13, 2017

Bill picked me up at Hannah's and we drove to Calvary to Dan Farnsworth's to pick up the ELF. Dan is not a young man. I think he is about

80 years old. His wife is in the nursing home. He has his hands full with her. Besides that, he buys and sells hay.

We got the bike loaded and tarped it with a tarp I had bought in Greenville. We drove back to Hannah's house. We got there about two in the afternoon. I told Bill that we could leave at midnight. He agreed and went home to get some sleep. At midnight, here he was. Well, now another very hard goodbye. That's life!

Tuesday, March 15, 2017

We got to Durham at about 8:30 in the morning. I had heard that Organic Transit had moved. We found the new location. It wasn't far from the old location. It wasn't nearly as nice. There was a big, tall fence around it with a sign saying that they wouldn't be open until 9 am. We sat there and waited until someone came and unlocked the gate. I guess I was a surprise for them. I didn't call them to tell them that I was coming.

Somewhere along the way, we realized that the tarp was all ripped and the back window on the bike was all broken up. Actually, it was kind of sad, but it made me laugh because it looked so bad. We tied the tarp back on the best we could and went on our way.

We unloaded the ELF and put it in front of the gate. When the first person came, they could see it and look for us. Once we got in the gate, Bill went on his way. He stopped at his family's and got some sleep. I told the mechanic my sad story. They worked me in as they had time. I had contacted Wendy in Cary and told her that I would be there on Tuesday. Wendy works at Target from 8 am until 3 pm.

Rob Cotter, the inventor of the ELF, stopped by during the day. I talked to him and told him my sad story. We'll take care of it. In the afternoon, Wendy and Bill picked me up and took me to their home in Cary. A week later, they called me to tell me my bike was ready to go. They had overhauled it and then some. I stayed one more night in Cary.

Tuesday, April 11, 2017

When I left Cary, I followed my route for the third time. I hadn't been to Clinton, N.C. I am not sure how I got there. I just kind of stopped to get some copies of literature that I handed out along the way. I asked if they knew a Lion and if there was a motel nearby. The clerk in the store gave me the number of a Lion and I gave him my phone number. I rode off to find the motel.

I found one and checked in. I made myself comfortable. The sun was shining, as I was sitting in the doorway. My phone was ringing. I answered it. It was Lion Catherine Young. She had gone in the store after I left. They gave her my phone number. After I talked to her and I told her that I was in a motel and where, she came to see me right away. She told me that I could come tomorrow to the Hurricane Church and stay there.

Wednesday, April 12, 2017

I met Catherine at the church. They had a huge building next to the church that was like a rescue storm shelter for the community. It was set up with a kitchen and everything else. Attached to this building was another big building housing tractors and a small bus to pick people up for church. They had mattresses and blankets and whatever else sitting around. I made myself at home. It was very cozy for me in there.

Easter was going to be that weekend. That was good. I'll stay for Easter right next to the church. I spent most of my time in the town of Clinton. One day, I was requested to visit the car dealership. All the customer that came thought that they were selling that contraption.

Another day, I was invited to go to a grade school in the neighboring town of Joanna. Eddie Marshall, the Principal, also a Lion, invited me.

Easter was great. They had a big meal where I was staying. The men of the church came very early in the morning to prepare the meal. Of course, I helped all I could. I was living there.

Monday, April 17, 2017

I rode my bike to Clinton and stayed with Lion Sharon Bumgardner one night. I met her family. I had a great time.

I looked at the map and measured it out. Traveling 40 miles a day, I could make it back to Rochester, Minnesota in six months. I had made plans to go through Chicago to go to the Lions International Convention and ride the ELF in the parade at the convention. Little did I know what was in store for me.

Wednesday, April 19, 2017

I found a motel and that was good because it was raining. I checked in.

Thursday, April 20, 2017

I rode around in Spartanburg, South Carolina. As usual, I talked to a lot of people. I scoped out where the convention was going to be. Spartanburg is a big city. There was one short street with not much traffic on it. Some young man was going past me in his car on the other side of the street. He turned around and was looking at my contraption when, BANG, he hit the fire hydrant pretty hard. I felt so bad for him. He was a very nice young man. He said, "Don't worry. My girlfriend works at the hospital. It's my hyperactivity that made me do it." He drove his car into a parking lot. He said he couldn't drive it anymore. I couldn't give him a ride on my ELF. I felt sooo bad. I don't know what he ended up doing. I am so sorry, young man!

Friday, April 21, 2017

Lions Catherine and Allen came to the South Carolina State Lions Convention here in Spartanburg. They had a room with two beds. They told me I could sleep in one of the two beds. They had slept together for all these years and they aren't going to stop now. That was a huge motel for the convention. I had a good time, like always.

Monday, April 24, 2017

I am in a town called Easley. It was raining again, on and off like the day before. At that time, it was raining quite a bit. It doesn't bother me very much. I can ride anyway. I had stopped in a shopping area and was just looking around. A young man, his name was Nate, stopped to talk to talk to me. He wanted to interview me. I asked him if he was a reporter? "No" he said, "I am just very interested in what you are doing. Let's go in the coffee shop." We did and, in the process, he invited me to his friend's house. He escorted me to this beautiful home, on the edge of town. I was a little bit embarrassed, because I didn't have him call before we went there and would his friend's wife mind? It all was okay. They are all very young and they were very nice to me.

Tuesday, April 25, 2017

I rode to Pendleton, South Carolina. I stopped at a restaurant. A lady was just coming out of the restaurant. She came to see what I was crawling out of. Well, again, we got into conversation. She told me that the restaurant was closing. As we visited further, she invited me to come to her house if I didn't mind sleeping on a couch. She would drive ahead and I should follow her.

It was quite a ways to her house. I don't know how far, but I made it. I don't know how I can always be so lucky and find people like that. Her husband had died. They were in the process of moving. She had two houses. The next day we went to her other house, a much bigger house with all kinds of stairs. She had a lot of plants at that place. On Saturday, we went to some kind of flea market with all of her plants and other stuff. I was glad I could be of some help and have fun at the same time.

I met her daughter and son-in-law. We went to their house. It was a very big, beautiful house. I said something about my bike. (There was something wrong with it, but I don't remember what it was.) Her son-in-law was an avid bike rider and he knew the guy from a bike shop. Well, here we go again. After work, they came to Cathy's and worked on my ELF. It took them three evenings to get it fixed, and then, of course, no charge, again.

Monday, May 1, 2017

I have been on my journey for two years now. This was going to be the END of my journey. It is a good thing I extended it for six months. I had no idea what was going to happen.

Tuesday, May 2, 2017

I am leaving Cathy's. I am not going into the goodbyes.

I am going to Hartwell, Georgia. I have no connections there.

Thursday, May 4, 2017

I knew Terry Sarec when we both worked nights at Madonna Towers. She had told me where she had moved to from Rochester and said, if I got near where she lived, I could stay with her and her husband, Matt. I had her address, so I went there. I stayed at their house two nights. Terry had followed me on Facebook, so she knew when I got to their area. We had a great time visiting.

Sunday, May 7, 2017

I stayed in East Atlanta in a motel. Sunday morning, I left and went through the middle of Atlanta. I had no problem. When there are stop lights all the way through, I have no problem. I can keep up with the traffic, especially on Sunday morning. I rode to Dallas, GA. They are supposed to have a motel there. I rode around and around. Finally, I stopped at a house. Well, as luck would have it, they looked in the phone book for a Lions club. As luck would have it, again, they found a Lion and called her. Lion Ginger came and escorted me to her house. They had a meeting Monday night. I stayed for that. I left Ginger's on Tuesday. She sent me to her friend, Shirley's in Cedartown. The people are always great. I have to just keep repeating myself.

Shirley helped me get onto a bike trail into Alabama.

Alabama 2

The roads I traveled in Alabama

Wednesday, May 10, 2017

The first 30 miles into Alabama were heavenly. It was a very nice day. I could see that the next 10 miles hadn't been used much at all, and I figured out why. I got to a very steep hill and the road was rough. I peddled like crazy and had the power set at the max, and, at that, I barely moved but still, I made it. If I wouldn't have made it, I don't know what

I would have done. Thank God I did. I saw nobody the whole stretch. I ended up in Anniston, Alabama. I found a motel right away. I called my friend, Pedro, whom I had met when I went through Alabama the first time. I just wanted him to know I was back in Alabama.

Thursday, May 11, 2017

I got up early, as usual, checked out and went down the road to McDonald's. It wasn't long before I was sitting with a group of people. I found out that there was a Lions club and they had a meeting that day at noon and it wasn't very far from where I was. After visiting about three hours at McDonalds, I finally left to try to find where the Lions meeting would be. I stopped because I wanted to mail a thank you card. I got out of my bike and my feet didn't really want to cooperate. I had trouble finding the letter I had written. I found it and about at that time the mailman stopped. I gave him the letter. My words wouldn't come out quite right. I knew something was going on. I thought all I really needed was some orange juice. I couldn't really think straight anymore. I think I wrote in the story about my health that I am opposite of a diabetic. I thought that I had low sugar in my blood. But, at that time, I could not think quite right. I went into one of the businesses. I told them that I was having trouble. She told me to sit on the couch. Then she came over to help me. I was looking through my remedies. I could not find one to take when I think I am going to have a stroke. I had the lady call my daughter, but she didn't answer her phone. Now that I look back, all I needed was orange juice and water. They called the ambulance, which was located right behind the building. Of course, they were right there. They took my blood pressure. It was sky high. They took me to the hospital. The Doctor came in and said, "If you are having a stroke, we have to helicopter you to Birmingham. Every minute counts." I signed some papers. I mostly just drew a line and they loaded me up in the helicopter. I never lost consciousness.

In Birmingham, they took all kinds of tests and found nothing, except that I had a urinary tract infection. When I had time, I called Pedro and told him what happened and that I was in Birmingham in the hospital. He and his wife came right away. They were thinking of letting me go that afternoon, but the doctors were not there to give the go-ahead. I will have to stay here until tomorrow.

Friday, May 12, 2016

This whole episode stopped me in my tracks. Pedro and his wife came today and picked me up. My ELF was taken care of by one of the businesses. They took it to their home.

I called my home in Chatfield and told them to come and pick me up. It so happened that Janelle's brother, Doug, was visiting from Iowa. Janelle's husband, Kevin, was in so much pain in his hip that he couldn't drive. Doug had time, so he drove Janelle and Kevin to get me. Doug drove all the way. They stopped overnight one night. They picked me up on Saturday and we drove to Anniston to get the ELF loaded.

I guess it all worked out the way it was supposed to. It wasn't meant for me to ride my bike in the parade at the Lions International Convention. I say, "It is all okay!"

A very big thank you to Faye and Pedro! And, also, to Janelle, Kevin and Doug. That will be something never forgotten.

Faye and Pedro

Closing

Thanks for going on my journey with me as you read my book.

If you have a dream, set a date. If it is years from now, still set a date. If you change it, it's okay.

Keep dreaming

PEACE, LOVE and HOPE

Hanna